HOW TO OBTAIN MAXIMUM COLLEGE FINANCIAL AID

4TH EDITION

by Edward Rosenwasser

**STUDENT COLLEGE AID PUBLISHING DIVISION
7950 N. STADIUM DRIVE # 229
HOUSTON, TEXAS 77030**

Copyrighted 1994
ISBN 0-932495-08-7

This book may not be reproduced in any part or form by any process, including incorporation into data retrieval systems, without written consent of the publisher. Violation of this provision will be vigorously prosecuted.

All information in this book is to the best of our knowledge current and correct. Student College Aid cannot guarantee its accuracy.

Editorial correspondence to:
Student College Aid
7950 N. Stadium Drive #229
Houston, TX 77030

Bookstore inquiries to:
Login Publications Consortium
Ben Woodworth
312-939-0959

ABBREVIATION ii

PREFACE TO FIRST EDITION iii

PREFACE TO SECOND EDITION v

PREFACE TO THIRD EDITION vi

PREFACE TO FOURTH EDITION (IMPORTANT TO READ) viii

1 THE FIRST STEP 1
2 START EARLY FILLING IN THE FORM 5
3 SPECIAL CONDITIONS FOR INDEPENDENT STUDENTS 30
4 INCOME 33
5 OTHER INCOME 39
6 COMPUTATION OF TAXES ON FORMS 43
7 FINISHING THE APPLICATION FORM 44
8 CORRECTIONS TO APPLICATION DATA 48
9 THE MOST USED AWARDS 50
10 CAMPUS-BASED PROGRAMS 57
11 LOAN CONSOLIDATION 89
12 HOW TO INCREASE GOVERNMENTAL FINANCIAL AID 93
13 STATE GRANTS 96
14 NON-GOVERNMENTAL LOANING SOURCES 102
15 FOR THE MORE AFFLUENT 121
16 SPECIAL FEDERAL SCHOLARSHIP 125
17 MILITARY SCHOLARSHIPS 127
18 HEALTH EDUCATION PROGRAMS 129
19 MILITARY MEDICAL PROGRAMS 135
20 MINORITY PROGRAMS 136
21 VETERANS PROGRAMS 138
22 MORE UNDERGRADUATE SOURCES 139
23 GRADUATE AWARDS 149
24 POTPOURRI 151
25 COOPERATIVE EDUCATION - AN OVERVIEW 169
APPENDIX A: STATE INFORMATION AGENCIES 204

ABBREVIATIONS

ACT-American College Testing
ADC-Aid to Dependent Children
AFDC-Aid to Families with Dependent Children
AFSA-Application for Federal Student Aid
AFSSA-Application for Federal and State Student Aid
ANCSA-Alaska Native Claims Settlement Act
CSS-College Scholarship Service
DEA-Dependents Educational Assistance
DEAE-Division of Educational and Agency Evaluation
DIC-Dependency Indemnity Compensation
EFC-Expected Family Contribution
FAF-Financial Aid Form
FAO-Financial Aid Officer
FC-Family Contribution
FFS-Family Financial Statement
FFELP-Federal Financial Education Loan Program
FWS-Federal Work Study
HEA-Higher Education Act
ICL-Income Contingent Loans
ISSC-Illinois State Scholarship Commission
JTPA-Job Training Partnership Act
MDE-Multiple Data Entry(companies processing the FAF, ACT, etc.)
NDSL-National Direct Student Loan
PHEAA-Pennsylvania Higher Education Assistance Agency
PLUS-Parents Loans for Undergraduate Students
SAI-Student Aid Index
SAR-Student Aid Report
SEOG-Supplemental Education Opportunity Act
FSLS-Federal Supplemental Loans for Students
SS-Social Security
SSIG-State Student Incentive Grant
UM-Uniform Methodology

PREFACE TO FIRST EDITION

The federal and state governments contribute more to college education than any single nongovernmental source. Therefore, if possible, the student should try to qualify for these funds.

In order to qualify the applicant must undergo a Need Analysis. This is a formula used to determine the ability of the family and/or applicant to pay college costs. The parental and student income and assets are plugged into this formula. This formula produces a sum called the FAMILY CONTRIBUTION. This sum, when subtracted from the cost of college, indicates the NEED.

NEED does not mean you are needy. It is merely a number obtained by arithmetic manipulation of the parents' and student's income and assets. One of the purposes of this book is to suggest to you the most advantageous way to honestly arrive at income and assets.

Who does this NEED ANALYSIS? Mainly, there are two companies, American College Testing Program (ACT) and College Scholarship Service (CSS).

The Colleges themselves vary in their cost, the amount and mix (scholarships, loans and work-study jobs) of funds that they will allot to the student. The student should investigate this by contacting the various schools. Some schools are anxious to increase their enrollment; others would like to decrease the student population. A desire to enlarge is often reflected in their willingness to help with finances. You can negotiate most successfully with high grades and high SAT scores.

No matter what route the financing of a college education may take, early planning will help ensure that you will not end up paying more than you should, nor will you have to make a last minute change in the college of your choice.

Age, whether too young or too old, is not a qualifier in applying for college or vocational school governmental aid. Acceptance to the institution allows you to apply for this aid.

Some people dislike using loans to go to school because the money must be repaid. However, going to college is an investment. It is estimated a college education will mean $450,000 more in income over a 30 year working career. Using loan money, interest free during your college career and having over ten years to repay the loan, appears to me to be an excellent investment.

The information that follows is pertinent to both undergraduate and graduate students: keep an eye out for the factors that will affect you.

PREFACE TO SECOND EDITION

In the Fall of 1986, Congress changed the law concerning Governmental Aid for college and vocational students. Mainly, the federal cutoff point is lower for determining eligibility for educational grants and loans. That is, families of applicants must now have lower incomes and assets than were previously required. So middle income families have to be more knowledgeable and inventive in order to qualify for grants and loans.

One way, before the Fall of '86, to qualify for more money for school was to be an independent student. The independent student has far less income and assets than his/her parents; therefore, he/she is able to receive more funding. Uncle Sam changed the criteria for being classified as an independent student; now, instead of an income/asset dependency requirement, there is an age or military service requirement. There are other factors determining one's classification as an independent student which are also included in the new legislation, and these will be discussed in detail below.

Assets are also described in detail. Later in the book we discuss what to do with them so they won't work against you. Be aware that negatives can work in your favor, such as when your house is worth less than you owe on it.

I have also included a great deal of information about income. No need to read it all; only the parts that apply to you. It is difficult to hide income, but a change in income is helpful to your cause. Also, you will see how to treat sale of business or farm assets due to foreclosure, forfeiture, bankruptcy, or liquidation.

The purpose of all this material is to allow you to qualify for as much governmental financial aid as is possible for you, to do it correctly the first time so as to obtain the funds while they are available, to borrow money most inexpensively, to pay for college with before-tax money, and to finance both graduate and undergraduate education.

Do it early and do it correctly. Normally, if you submit your financial aid forms after March 1st, you lose available aid. This is an instance of the early bird getting the worm. Use this book as a reference for each school year that you attend school.

PREFACE TO THIRD EDITION

Please read preface one and two. Number one in particular abstracts how the system works. The first 8 chapters of this edition deal with completing the financial aid forms correctly so you will obtain the maximum of the awards in the next 15 chapters. I constructed a small index to cover topics in the last 16 chapters.

Social and economic behavior are influenced by our laws. Though much has been said and written about service to the community being used to earn payment for college, as of this writing Congress has passed the law, but appropriated no money.

What has occurred is that the option to have a student classified as independent, by the student working to earn $4,000 a year and not being claimed as a tax deduction by the parents, has been eliminated. Moreover, not all Guaranteed Student Loans are interest free, but the interest rate is lower than in the preceding years.

One way to reduce the amount of loans for college is to work part time, not at the minimum wage, but at an adequate wage. It normally takes a year longer to graduate using this method, but you have had the experience of working in your field, you most likely will have a better than entry level job waiting for you on graduation and you owe far less in loans. We explain all about this in a new section called "Cooperative Education".

So many people try to find the name of the company from whom they borrowed money, that we have included an appendix for this purpose. Some students fail to keep records of such loans. When the students leave school the loaning institution has no way to contact them. Then the student receives a notice from a collection agency, and this company wants all the loan and interest NOW! Next the IRS garnishes any tax refunds and your credit is impaired. If you are not paying off your school loans, use the appendix to make contact with your creditor and save yourself a bunch of headaches.

There is information in the book that explains how the new laws are trying to limit loan defaults.

I thought the information about the National Early Intervention Scholarship And Partnership Program was so important for students down the pike, that I included a good bit of information. Parents with smaller children should read this section.

Information about proprietary schools, schools whose purpose is not only to educate, but to also make a profit, takes up much more space in this edition. Some clients are very contented with their proprietary school education, others feel they have been left with financial burdens and no education in return. If you are considering this type of education, read this section under the heading POTPOURRI. Go by the standards enumerated, not by a sale pitch as "the Harvard of the proprietary schools."

Under this same chapter is information from the HEA Amendments about campus security. Not only should all female students read this section, but all male students as well. We are referring here to sexual crimes. There is nothing more costly, emotionally and financially, than to be assaulted. One's boundaries are voided, and it takes some time for them to grow back again.

Like always the up to date information about governmental college aid is elucidated with the target being that the student will get their maximum share of financial aid, preferably scholarships. There also are new scholarships explained.

Some while back I read an interview with John Pierce, the famous electrical engineer who is responsible to a major degree for satellite communications. When he entered Cal Tech as a freshman he was a chem engineer major. He had chosen this field because the only scientist, his friend's father, he knew was a chemical engineer. After the first year he knew he couldn't hack chemistry. No matter how talented one is, certain subjects don't turn them on. He looked for another major and luckily found his niche in electrical engineering.

In other words going to college could be a bumpy road. I hope we have somewhat smoothed the financial side.

PREFACE TO FOURTH EDITION

Since the changes between the 3rd and 4th edition are not major, and in order to lower the selling price of this book, changes are described in this preface and are referenced to the appropriate page.

See page 89 for Federal Consolidation Loans

Eligible borrower

The requirement that the borrower must consolidate at least $7,500 in eligible student loans has been deleted. This change takes effect for Federal Consolidation Loans disbursed on or after July 1, 1994.

Income-sensitive repayment

If a borrower certifies to a lender that, on or after July 1, 1994, he or she has sought, but has been unable to obtain a Federal Consolidation Loan with an income-sensitive repayment schedule from the holders of the loans that the borrower wishes to consolidate, then any other Federal Consolidation Loan lender may make a Federal Consolidation Loan to that borrower. Regulations prescribing the rules to be used for establishing income-sensitive repayment schedules for all FFEL Program loans (except Federal PLUS Loans) are currently being developed through negotiated rule making.

Repayment provisions

1. The interest rate on a Federal Consolidation Loan disbursed on or after July 1, 1994 shall be the weighted average of the interest rates on the loans consolidated, rounded upward to the nearest whole percent. These loans will not have a minimum interest rate of 9 percent.

2. If the amount of the Federal Consolidation Loan is less than $7,500, the borrower's repayment schedule may not exceed 10 years. This charge applies to Federal Consolidation Loans disbursed on or after July 1, 1994.

Terms and conditions

1. The provision entitling a Federal Consolidation Loan borrower to an interest subsidized deferment has been deleted, except for a borrower who receives a Federal Consolidation Loan that discharges only subsidized Federal Stafford Loans. This change is effective for Federal Consolidation Loans made based on applications received by an eligible lender on or after August 10, 1993. Any borrower who is currently eligible for interest subsidies on a Federal Consolidation Loan will remain eligible for those benefits.

2. A borrower may also obtain a Direct Federal Consolidation Loan from the Secretary on or after July 1, 1994, if the Secretary determines that the Department of Education has the necessary origination and servicing arrangements in place for such loans. In order for a borrower who does not have an FDSL Program loan to obtain a Direct Federal Consolidation Loan from the Secretary, the borrower must certify that he or she has been unable to obtain a Federal Consolidation Loan or a Federal Consolidation Loan with income-sensitive repayment terms from an FFEL Program lender.

Variable Interest rate beginning July 1, 1994

The variable interest rate on a Federal PLUS Loan for which the first disbursement is made on or after July 1, 1994 shall be determined on June 1 of each year and shall apply to the 12-month period beginning July 1 and ending on June 30. The Secretary shall determine the interest rate by adding 3.1 percent to the bond equivalent rate of 52-week Treasury bills auctioned at the final auction held prior to such June 1, except that the interest rate shall not exceed 9 percent.

Variable interest rate beginning July 1, 1998

The variable interest rate on a Federal PLUS Loan for which the first disbursement is made on or after July 1, 1998 shall be determined on June 1 of each year and shall apply to the 12-month period beginning July 1 and ending on June 30. The Secretary shall determine the interest rate by adding 2.1 percent to the bond equivalent rate of the securities with a comparable maturity, as established by the Secretary after consultation with the Secretary of the Treasury, except that the interest rate shall not exceed 9 percent.

See page 74 +

Unsubsidized Federal Stafford Loan limits

1. The annual and aggregate limits for unsubsidized Federal Stafford Loans made to a dependent undergraduate student shall be the same as the annual and aggregate subsidized Federal Stafford Loan applicable to such student. This change will become effective for loans first disbursed on or after July 1, 1994 for periods of enrollment that either include that date or begin after that date.

2. For any other student, the loan limits shall be (1) the annual and aggregate subsidized Federal Stafford Loan limits applicable to such student, less the amount of any subsidized Federal Stafford Loan received by the student plus (2) the annual and aggregate loan limits. For example, a first-year independent undergraduate student who qualified for, and received a $1,000 subsidized Federal Stafford Loan, could borrow up to an additional $5,625 unsubsidized Federal Stafford Loan $1,625 remaining under the freshman limit plus $4,000 under the FFEL available to the student. This change will become effective for loans first disbursed on or after July 1, 1994 for periods of enrollment that either include that date or begin after that date.

/Unsubsidized Federal Stafford Loan repayment period

1. The borrower's repayment period for an unsubsidized Federal Stafford Loan begins on the date the first payment of principal is due from the borrower. This change will become effective for loans first disbursed on or after July 1, 1994 for periods of enrollment that either include that date or begin after that date.

2. The amount of the borrower's periodic payment and the length of the repayment schedule shall be established by assuming an interest rate equal to the applicable rate of interest at the time the repayment of principal is scheduled to begin. At the option of the lender, the promissory note or other written evidence of the loan may require that the amount of the periodic payment will be adjusted annually, or the length of the repayment period will be adjusted to accommodate variable interest rate changes. The Secretary will revise the common application/promissory note to accommodate this option. This change will become effective for loans first disbursed on or after July 1, 1994 for

periods of enrollment that either include that date or begin after that date.

Unsubsidized Federal Stafford Loan origination fee

Before the enactment of Pub. L 103-66, the lender was required to charge the borrower a 6.5 percent "origination fee/insurance premium." This fee has been renamed as simply the "origination fee," and the amount has been reduced to 3 percent of the principal amount of a loan first disbursed on or after July 1, 1994 for a period of enrollment that either includes that date or begins after that date. In addition, the guaranty agency may charge the borrower an insurance premium that does not exceed 1 percent of the principal amount of the loan, in accordance with *428H(l), effective for loans first disbursed on or after July 1, 1994 for periods of enrollment that either include that date or begin after that date.

Variable interest rate beginning July 1, 1994

The variable interest rate on a Federal Stafford Loan shall be determined on June 1 of each your and shall apply to the 12-month period beginning July 1 and ending on June 30. The Secretary shall determine the interest rate by adding 3.1 percent to the bond equivalent rate of 90-day Treasury bills auctioned at the final auction held prior to such June 1, except that the interest rate shall not exceed 8.25 percent. This change will become effective for loans first disbursed on or after July 1, 1994 for periods or enrollment that either include that date or begin after that date.

Variable interest rate beginning July 1, 1995

During the borrower's in-school, grace, and deferment periods, the variable interest rate on a Federal Stafford Loan shall be determined on June 1 or each year and shall apply to the 12-month period beginning July 1 and ending on June 30. The Secretary shall determine the interest rate by adding 2.5 percent to the bond equivalent rate of 91-day Treasury bills auctioned at the final auction held prior to such June 1, except that the interest rate shall not exceed 8.25 percent. This change will become effective for loans first disbursed on or after July 1, 1995 for periods of enrollment that either include that date or begin after that date.

Variable interest rate beginning July 1, 1998

The variable interest rate on a Federal Stafford Loan shall be determined on June 1 of each year and shall apply to the 12-month period beginning July 1 and ending on June 30. The Secretary shall determine the interest rate by adding 1 percent to the bond equivalent rate of the securities with a comparable maturity, as established by the Secretary after consultation with the Secretary of the Treasury, except that the interest rate shall not exceed 8.25 percent. This change will become effective for loans first disbursed on or after July 1, 1998 for periods of enrollment that either include that date or begin after that date.

See pages 69 & 74

Elimination of Federal SLS Program

The Federal SLS Program has been merged into the unsubsidized component of the Federal Stafford Loan Program, and will no longer exist as a separate program. No new Federal SLS Loans may be made for a period of enrollment beginning on or after July 1, 1994. All conditions and benefits applicable to existing Federal SLS Loans will continue for those loans. Also, to the extent that current unsubsidized Federal Stafford Loans have different conditions and benefits that under the merged program, those loans retain those different conditions and benefits.

1 THE FIRST STEP

A SIMPLE ACTION WILL GET YOU STARTED!

The first step in obtaining college financial aid is to inquire at the Financial Aid Office of the schools you are interested in attending and ask if they participate in the various federal and state financial aid programs. Have them give or mail you this information. Keep a list of which programs each school participates in and the filing deadline for each semester or quarter.

Also request that the school send you the appropriate forms for you to apply for financial aid. If you are applying to several schools that use the same form, there are spaces on the form to indicate the various schools that should receive the information, and you will only have to fill that form out once.

If you need financial assistance for college, and if the school you are considering attending does not offer such assistance or offers less than other schools, you might think about attending another school. Pick the school that is best for you which you can afford.

In certain academic or vocational fields some schools are considered more prestigious than others by certain employers. If these schools are within your academic ranking, expense should not be a prohibiting constraint.

Academic ranking is considered for entrance into colleges. A 2.0 (C) average is necessary to continue federal and state financial aid, and some non-governmental scholarships require a 2.5 or higher average. You should not feel badly if you cannot obtain these averages. Perseverance, drive and non-academic talents are still in demand. Keep an open mind, become involved in something and you will find or create your own niche. But whatever you do, don't get down on yourself. As Shakespeare had Hamlet say, "There's nothing good or bad, but thinking doeth make it so."

When calculating college cost, six elements are considered. 1) Tuition and fees. These are approximately the same for all students at the same school. These amounts are usually higher for out of state students. 2) Books and supplies. These costs depend on the courses you are taking. 3) Housing. The expense depends on where you live, whether in a dorm, an apartment or at home. 4) Meals. This expense also depends on where you live. 5) Personal Expense. This includes clothes and their maintenance, health insurance, auto expense (if you have a car), toiletry items etc. If the student is physically handicapped or if the student has child care bills, personal expense may be set very high. 6) Transportation. This item is also variable. It may include commuting costs or three round trip air coach fares to a distant home.

Everyone, rich, poor and in between, can benefit from completing these financial aid forms. The Government has lowered the amount of income you can earn to qualify for a Pell Grant it provides for scholarships and has increased the amount it provides for low interest and long term payback loans. These loans are available only if the FAF or other such forms have been completed. Private scholarships should be sought to control the loan debt.

THE COST OF A COLLEGE EDUCATION

Presently, the cost of a four year college education runs between $28,000 and $120,000. Costs of between $42,000 and $60,000 are typical. Next to your home, this may be the single most expensive investment you make, especially if you have more than one child to educate.

HOW IS ELIGIBILITY FOR COLLEGE FINANCIAL AID DETERMINED?

To determine if your family is eligible for college financial aid, a Financial Aid Form (FAF) must be completed and submitted to the College Scholarship Service of Princeton, New Jersey, or some colleges require the ACT form (Academic College Testing of Des Mones, IA), but the procedure is the same. The information you provide on this form is carefully examined by the College Scholarship Service to determine the amount you can reasonably afford to contribute toward college expenses. This may or may not be the amount you can actually afford. College financial aid is available only to the extent that actual college expenses exceed this calculated amount.

Once this determination is made, the results are sent directly to the financial aid officer(s) of the college(s) selected by the prospective student. The college financial aid officer then determines the types of financial assistance to offer the student.

NEW RULES FROM 1992 AMENDMENTS OF HEA

Throughout the rest of this book you are informed of the new rules and programs in the 1992 amendments and subsequent measures. Of course Congress often does not appropriate funds for programs it authorizes. Check with your financial aid counselor.

Be aware that when the word "Secretary" is used, it refers to the Secretary of Education.

Since the 1992 Amendments to the HEA there is now a single Title IV Federal aid application that is free to all applicants.

If someone other than the applicant completes the form on the applicant's behalf, then that individual must provide his or her name, signature, address, social security number, and organizational affiliation.

Only the data collected on the federal financial aid form may be used in determining a student's need. The HEA provides that the Secretary of Education assist states and institutions in collecting data for State and institutional aid. In addition a separate identifiable loan application that students or institutions must submit directly to eligible lenders is provided by the FFEL Program,

STUDENT ELIGIBILITY - ABILITY-TO-BENEFIT

A student who does not have a high school diploma or its recognized equivalent is eligible to receive Title IV student financial assistance only if:

1. The student takes an independently administered examination

approved by the Secretary of Education and achieves a score specified by the Secretary that demonstrates the student can benefit from the education or training being offered; or

2. The student is determined to have the ability-to-benefit from the education or training being offered in accordance with a process prescribed by the state in which the institution the student is attending is located. The HEA provides that any such process shall become effective 6 months after it is submitted to the Secretary unless it is disapproved by the Secretary. In approving that process, the Secretary will take into account the effectiveness of the process in enabling those students to benefit from the instruction offered and the cultural diversity, economic circumstances, and educational preparation of the populations served.

This provision does not apply to the Federal SLS Program, because a student must have a high school diploma or its recognized equivalent to be eligible to borrow under that program.

2 START EARLY FILLING IN THE FORM

GETTING STARTED

You will need last year's tax return for the income, medical expense and tax figures. If you have nontaxable income, you will need these figures also. You will also need asset information.

If this form is to be completed before your income tax return is completed, then you must estimate your figures. How close must you be? Normally within $200 on any single item or the total on all items must not exceed $400 misjudgment. If you surpass this, the estimate may not be accepted, and then it must be recalculated and this takes time. As soon as the tax form is completed the exact figures should be submitted on the acknowledgement form provided in response to your initial submission.

These forms are read by scanning devices; therefore, write, print or type as neatly and clearly as possible. If you have questions about a specific inquiry, call a financial aid officer at a college in your community. This will save a long distance call. Otherwise, call the company that produces the forms or the federal information number 1-(800)4FED AID.

It is best not to leave blanks. Fill in with 0, no, or N/A; whichever is more applicable.

Don't forget, have all the necessary signatures on the form, and mail to the address on the form only. You must avoid mistakes in order for your forms to be processed in time to share in the available moneys.

Let me give you some words of caution. Some schools screen your inquiries over the phone or in person with people who are not fully trained in answering your questions. Try to speak to a regular financial aid counselor or to the head of the department. You can also call the federal information number which is 1-800-433-3243.

ACKNOWLEDGEMENT FORM

Some weeks after you have mailed your completed application you will receive an acknowledgement form. This lists, in abbreviated fashion, the information you originally submitted. If you note any errors you should so indicate and return the form.

Another part of this form will indicate the Family Contribution. This is the calculated value of the figures entered originally. This is the amount the processor, using the government's formula, calculates you are able to contribute to your child's education.

Let's suppose the results say you must contribute all the necessary funds. Some states have a low interest loan program that allows the family to now borrow all of the total contribution. More about this later.

This same information is sent to the financial aid officers at the schools you indicated on your original form. Your form is received along with hundreds or thousands of other forms.

THE AWARD LETTER

Still later the student will receive through the mail from the college an award letter. This letter will indicate the expense budget that has been developed for the student. It will state the amount the family and student must contribute towards the student's educational expense, and the amount and kinds of funds the school can supply. The letter will also ask if the student accepts these awards. You may accept all, part or none of these, but you must reply by the date indicated in the letter, if you hope to get aid from that school. Just because you accept the aid package does not mean you must attend that school.

The amount and type of aid may differ from school to school. Included in each letter you receive will be instructions for appealing any data in the letter with which you disagree. How successful you will be in your appeal depends on several factors, but appealing in no way jeopardizes your current award.

One thing that determines your success in your appeal is your making your appeal early enough in the funding cycle so that your counselor has some leeway in switching funds. Other factors are: how much the school wants you as a student, whether the college has discretionary funds, whether there have been any changes in your financial situation, whether your special financial situation was made clear to and understood by the financial aid officer. Probably foremost in this procedure is how diplomatically and logically you present your case. You must show an understanding for the schools position and present your case so both parties are accommodated.

Perhaps you have applied to several schools. Suppose you have not heard from the school you really want to attend, but you have heard from other schools you have applied to. Should you delay replying to the award letter until you have heard from your favorite school? DEFINITELY NOT! Your favorite school may not come through, You will be left out in the cold, if you don't respond by the date on the award letter.

Laws change and the family size and finances may change, so don't expect your award to be the same each year.

FINANCIAL AID PACKAGES

Let's suppose the cost of the college is $9,000 per year. This includes tuition, room and board, transportation, books, and personal expenses. Now suppose the determination has been made that the amount you can reasonably contribute is $3,000. Then you will be awarded $6,000 in various types of aid, determined by your financial aid officer.

Your financial aid package can be made up of grants from the federal and state governments, administered through your Financial Aid Officer (FAO). These are the Pell Grant, State Student Incentive Grant and the Tuition Equalization Grant. The second group of federal sources which the FAO may have available are the SEOG (Supplemental Educational Opportunity Grant), Federal Stafford Loan (formerly Stafford Loan), Perkins Loan, and College Work Study (CWS). There are other loans available, but these normally are not included in the Financial Aid Package. We will write more about these later.

If you have searched for, found, applied for and received a scholarship or loan not in the above, then this too is incorporated in the award package.

THE PROBLEM WITH THE SELECTION PROCEDURE

Many families automatically assume that they are not eligible for aid and simply do not bother to file the FAF etc.

Of those families who do file most are unaware of the impact their income and assets have on their eligibility for aid.

It takes 4 to 10 weeks for the FAF to be processed. Families usually don't know the results until May or June. By then it is too late to seek nongovernmental aid.

The family contribution determined by the processor is often more than the family can afford.

CONSTRAINING FACTORS

The family's income and assets and the student's classification (dependent or independent), student's income and assets are the constraining factors for college governmental financial aid.

If you have one college student and your adjusted gross income is over $27,000 a year, or two or more college students and your adjusted gross income is over $30,000 a year, you will probably not qualify for federal grants. If your income is less than the above, but your total assets are equal to or greater than $30,000, you will not qualify for federal grants. But nonetheless you should apply. This will make you eligible for other sources of money.

THE TRUE VALUE OF COLLEGE AID

The value of the financial aid you receive for college depends on the tax bracket you are in. If you are in the 15% bracket every dollar of aid is $1.18 you don't need to earn. Or if you receive no aid then you need to earn $1.18 to supply the student $1.00.

If you are in the 28% bracket every dollar of aid is $1.40 you do not need to earn.

2 Start Early Filling In The Forms

What follows is the information that helps you maximize your financial aid. As you read the following, think of the applications to your own situation.

A WORD OF CAUTION -- CRIMINAL PENALTIES

The HEA continues to provide for specific criminal penalties (with increased dollar amounts for fines) for any person who knowingly and willfully:

1. Embezzles, misapplies, steals, or obtains by fraud, false statement, or forgery, or fails to refund any funds provided or insured under Title IV;

2. Makes any false statements, furnishes false information, or conceals any material information in connection with the assignment of a Title IV loan;

3. Makes an unlawful payment to induce a lender to make or acquire a loan under the FFEL Program; or

4. Destroys or conceals any record relating to the provision of Title IV assistance with intent to defraud the United States or to prevent the United States from enforcing any right obtained by subrogation.

The HEA adds that any person who attempts to carry out any of the above activities will be subject to the specific criminal penalties. The HEA also clarifies that a person's knowing and willful failure to pay refunds is subject to criminal penalties.

SOCIAL SECURITY NUMBER

There must be a social security number on the application in order to obtain Federal aid. It is gathered for skip-tracing purposes for the loan programs, and to seek eligibility for a Pell Grant. A request for a Pell Grant will not be completely prepared without the applicant's social security number. If an application form is turned in without a social security number, the student is given a phony number by the federal processor. Later, if the student supplies a social security number to the federal processor, an aid index can be provided and a cross reference is established in the system to furnish a trail for spotting the student's records.

The accuracy of the social security number on the applicant should be checked carefully to avoid delays.

The necessity of a social security number in the case of applicants who are residents of Palau, the Federated States of Micronesia, and the Marshall Islands is waived. These students should leave the social security number box blank; they will be identified by the code given in the space for state of legal residence.

VERIFICATION OF APPLICATION FORM

Verification requirements apply to campus-based and Stafford Loan applications as well as Pell Grant, beginning with the 1986-87 award year.

ESTIMATED AND OFFICIAL EXPECTED FAMILY CONTRIBUTION (EFC)

If all necessary information is provided on the aid application, the MDE (Multiple Data Entry) or Central Processor can produce official EFCs under the Congressional and Pell Grant methodologies. The authority for the MDEs to produce official SAI (Student Aid Index), upon which disbursements can be made, was new beginning 1988-89.

Official EFCs can only be calculated if the data on the student aid application is complete. Applications with incomplete or inconsistent data are rejected by the Central Processor, and the resultant SAR (Student Aid Report) contain no expected family contributions. The MDEs may, however, be able to calculate estimated FCs in these cases. An estimated FC may not be used for making disbursements, but may be used to estimate a student's aid package.

If the SAI is estimated (and therefore unofficial), the appropriate corrections must be made on Part 2 of SAR, and sent back to the Central Processor for reprocessing. The aid administrator may also use this process to obtain an official FC under Congressional Methodology, or may recalculate the FC himself or herself.

2 Start Early Filling In The Forms

SOME FACTS AND FIGURES

Each year there are over $100 billion of financial aid available to families who can establish the need for post secondary financial assistance. This aid comes in the form of federal, state, local, college and private scholarships, grants, loans, endowments and work study programs.

About five billion dollars in low interest federally subsidized loans for students go unused each year. Some students think, incorrectly, that they are not eligible; others don't want to go through the paperwork hassle and still others just don't realize that the money is there.

To qualify for federal college aid you must be at least a half-time student. For schools on a semester, quarter, or trimester plan you must take at least six semester or quarter hours per term to be a half time student. If your school uses clock hours to measure course programs, you must attend twelve course hours per week. For schools using a credit hour system, you must attend twelve semester hours or eighteen quarter hours each school year.

OBLIGATORY DATA TO STUDENTS

The dissemination of reliable data to students concerning the terms and circumstances of their packages is basic, if they are to correctly understand and accept obligations for the arrangements which they sign. Such data should include: 1) the charge of attendance, 2) procedure on refunds, 3) moneys expected from the student or the family, 4) programs from which the student is obtaining funds (kinds of aid contained in the package), 5) the part of aid which must be paid back (loans) or earned (work-study or other employment), 6) the charges (interest rate and other charges) on any loans, 7) repayment methods and deferment and/or cancellation provisos on any loan acquired as a part of the package, 8) data about the job assignment for a work-study award, 9) the payment calendar and method of making allocations to students, 10) how the school ascertains whether the student is making acceptable academic progress, and 11) what ensues if the student fails to make acceptable academic progress.

Students who are not eligible or whose full need has not been met should be informed of the reasons of such decisions and should be referred to alternative sources of funding.

LEARNING ABOUT THE ELEMENTS OF THE FAF OR ACT

Be aware of the following topics that apply to you in order to qualify for maximum college financial aid.

You do not need to read all of the sections that follow. Concern yourself only with those that are applicable to your situation.

ASSETS

The following are considered as assets:

1) Cash on hand, Checking,

2) Cash on hand, Savings,

3) Net value of business/farm less encumbrances,

4) Net value of other real estate less encumbrances,

5) Stocks/Bonds/Other Securities,

6) Money Market Funds,

7) All other investments.

Items 3 & 4 are valued in this manner: Suppose you had to sell your real property this very day. What would you get for it? Assume you don't have a chance to advertise or dicker. How much would you have to sacrifice on the price of this item? This is the proper value to enter for these items.

Any amount that you owe on or is secured by these items should be subtracted from these values. It is possible to have a negative value.

With the 1992 HEA amendments the house evaluation is no longer requested on the governmental form (the Federal Needs Analysis Methodology). Though this figure is no longer used in the calculations, some schools request and look at this figure in calculating the mix of your aid. If it is necessary to evaluate your home, it is done the same way as items 3 & 4 above.

Merrill Lynch has what is known as an equity access account. This account lets you borrow against the equity in your home. If the equity assets accounts are not available in your state, you can take a lien against your home to pay off the consumer debts (consumer debts are not considered in the evaluation process) and thereby lower the value of your home etc. No matter what you do you should figure the worst case scenario. For instance, if you borrow heavily against your home and suddenly you loose your job. Will you be able to handle this and not get into a financial bind?

IRS liens should not be counted against the value of the house. The "market" value is the price that would be put on the home if it were for sale as of the date the application for financial aid is filed, rather than the assessed value, the insured value, or the tax value. The "home" may be a house, a condominium, a mobile home, or other residence. Homes purchased under a land contract are also included.

HOME EQUITY LOANS

Home equity loans may legally be used to pay expenses such as home improvements and medical expenses. Parents who pay for college on a current basis may use this loan to pay tuition. There are some ceilings to a home equity loan's interest deductibility. Whatever the current estimated value, the total borrowed amount may not exceed the house's purchase price plus the cost of improvements. If you borrow more than the decreed limit, but use it only on educational costs (or medical costs), the deductibility is allowed.

Banks have their own ceilings. They will initiate a line of credit somewhere between 50 and 75 percent of the present market value of the home or condominium.

Home equity loans were popular due to the rapid rise in real estate values. Many homeowners desired to use the equity that had built up over the years. A different way of borrowing from your own assets is to remortgage your home. The traditional way is to take out a second mortgage if the first is not completely paid for. However, these are not changeable and are expensive. Interest rates can increase between 20 percent and 50 percent over the original mortgage.

Home equity loans were introduced to unleash the paper wealth in ones home, basically a line of credit against your home. A house worth $40,000 in 1970 was frequently worth $120,00 in the market a decade or so later. There are costs connected with opening this line of credit such as an appraiser's fee, a mortgage search, and an application processing fee. This could add 2 percent or more of the line of credit. In some cases, the fees are even higher.

The rate of interest is the most important factor for this type of loan. Mortgage lenders often insist on adjustable or variable rate loans. Interest rates on the loans are related to some general index such as Treasury bills, the prime rate, or the consumer price index. Loans that are bound to such indices are subject to interest rate changes, which can mean greater (or lesser) monthly payments. If the economy goes into a period of prolonged inflation, the higher interest rates could be painful. Usually interest rates will be in line with new mortgage rates, even 1 or 2 percent points higher.

I personally do not like calling grandparents into the educational fray. But since these are magnanimous people, I will list another option. Grandparents can use their homes to assist in college expenses by a type of mortgage called a reverse annuity mortgage. It is not yet available in every state. The reverse mortgage yields a monthly payment from the bank. The mortgage and monthly payments are tied to an annuity table. The owner retains the house until his or her death, then it returns to the bank. It is not cheap to set up, and the interest rate may be considerable. But it can give additional income and, if extra funds are available, assistance to a grandchild in school.

HOW ARE ASSETS EVALUATED

When ACT or CSS evaluate assets, the formula used says that 5.6% of the parents' assets are available for college costs. For example, if you show $5,000 in assets, the formula says you are able to contribute $280 of these assets to the college costs. If you have $30,000 in assets, you can contribute $1,680 to college costs.

If you own a business (sole proprietor), your assets are valued at 40% of net value up to a $55,000. Considering $30,000 as the value of your business, 40% of this is $12,000 (considered as an asset), so your expected contribution would be 5.6% of $12,000 or $672.

If you own 51% of a sub chapter S corporation and relatives own the other 49%, and if you have assets of $30,000, you can put these assets in the corporation. You would then be expected to contribute ($30,000 x 51% x 40% x 5.6% = $342.72

When assets are listed on the students account, it is considered that 33% of these are available for college costs. Consider a student with $1,000 in assets. The expected contribution would be $330, whereas; if those assets were in the parents' account, the expected contribution would be $56. So in some situations it may be more productive to have the student give the parents his or her assets. The author finds the idea of using a small business attractive.

It is difficult for us to grasp how much a trillion dollars is. It is similarly difficult to picture the vast size of the U.S. economy. If you can visualize one small niche that needs filling in this economy, then you're on your way with a small business of your own.

CASH, SAVINGS, AND CHECKING ACCOUNTS

The amount reported as cash, savings, and checking should be the amount on hand on the date the application is filed, excluding any amount which has been received from financial aid programs. This amount may not be updated to reflect changes occurring after the application has been filed.

Custodial accounts set up by parents or grandparents for an applicant are reported as an asset of the applicant. Joint bank accounts cannot be arbitrarily apportioned; if two people own the account, each reports 50%.

2 Start Early Filling In The Forms

A way to lower your assets is to purchase any large items (refrigerator, washing machine, etc.) you need before you list your assets. Paying for it lowers your checking or savings account.

OTHER REAL ESTATE AND INVESTMENTS

The current value of real estate (other than the home, farm, or business) plus any other investments should be recorded on the financial aid application. Amounts owed on the property listed or debts for which the property or investment was used as collateral is also listed.

Other real estate includes rental property, land, time-share property used for recreation, and second or summer homes. Personal and consumer debts should not be included in the amount owed on the property. If the value of the residential or commercial property is in doubt, the Housing Index Multiplier or Commercial Property Multiplier may be used as a guide. Deviations in value may result from location, damage to the property, or improvements.

Investments include, but are not limited to:

> money market funds;
>
> stocks, bonds, mutual funds, and other securities;
>
> certificates of deposit (CDs);
>
> installment and land sale contracts;
>
> commodities;
>
> precious and strategic metals;
>
> trust funds.

NOTE: Trust funds in the name of a specific individual, even though legally inaccessible to the eventual owner, should be included as part of the person's assets.

The value of retirement plans (pension funds, annuities, IRAs, Keogh accounts, etc.) are not to be reported as assets.

Assets represented by such investments as the holding of a take-back mortgage or the selling of property under a land contract are to be reported. However, there should be no debt reported on this type of asset. The asset will decrease each year depending on how much of the principle is paid back each year.

BUSINESS AND/OR FARM ASSETS

If the parents, or the applicant (and/or spouse), own a farm or business, the current market value of the farm or business must be indicated on the financial aid application. The value includes land, buildings, machinery, equipment, livestock, livestock products, crops, inventories, etc. If the home is on the farm, the value of the home should not be included in the farm value since it should already be entered separately under "home value." Any debts owed against the farm or business should be recorded only if the business or farm was used as collateral. If both a farm and a business are owned, their values are combined and reported in one entry; this is a change from applications in previous years.

If the parents or the applicant and spouse are not sole owner(s) of the farm or business, only their share in the ownership and their share of the debts against the business or farm should be listed. If this gets too involved, have your accountant help you.

FARM INCLUDED IN BUSINESS AND/OR FARM ASSETS

The need analysis formulas protect a portion of the combined farm and business assets. The amount protected is greater in the case of a farm than in the case of a business only; therefore, the parent or applicant must indicate if the amount reported includes farm assets.

AGE OF OLDER PARENT

The older parent's age controls the part of the assets protected for retirement. The older the parent is the greater the asset protection. If the age of the older parent is missing on the application, it is assumed to be

45 and, therefore, may cause a higher contribution.

AMERICAN INDIAN CLAIMS ACT

Funds received by Native Americans under the Alaska Native Claims or Maine Indian Claims Settlement Acts should not be reported as assets. Beginning with award year 1986-87, only assets resulting from payments in excess of $2,000 received under the Distribution of Judgment Funds Act or the Per Capita Act, should be reported as assets. Payments of $2,000 or less (regardless of the number of such payments received during the year) from these two acts should not be considered as assets. If any individual payment received was over $2,000, the excess held as assets must be reported.

NOTE: There is no longer an exclusion for property belonging to native Americans that is held in trust by the U.S. Government or that cannot be sold without consent of the Secretary of the Interior.

NEED ANALYSIS -- Effective for Award Years Beginning on or After July 1, 1993.

The 1992 Amendments supplant both the Congressional and Pell Grant Methodologies with a single statutory need analysis methodology to be used for determining the Expected Family Contribution (EFC) for all students applying for Title IV assistance. This methodology will be referred to as the Federal Needs Analysis Methodology.

The Federal Needs Analysis Methodology is generally based on the current Congressional Methodology, however, special treatment for dislocated workers and displaced homemakers has been abolish. Some of the highlights of the Federal Needs Analysis Methodology are as follows:

SIMPLIFIED NEED ANALYSIS FORMULA

The HEA authorizes the use of a simplified needs analysis formula for the determination of an EFC for a family with an adjusted family income of less than $50,000 which files an IRS form 1040A or 1040EZ or an income tax return required by the tax code of the Commonwealth of Puerto Rico,

2 Start Early Filling In The Forms

Guam, American Samoa, the U.S. Virgin Islands, the Republic of the Marshall Islands, the Federated States of Micronesia, or Palau, or is not required to file any income tax return. The simplified need analysis formula will use the following data elements:
- adjusted gross income
- federal income taxes paid
- untaxed income and benefits
- number of family members in the household
- number of family members in postsecondary education
- an allowance for state and other taxes.

AUTOMATIC ZERO EFC

The HEA provides that the parents of a dependent student or an independent student with dependents other than a spouse would be considered to have a zero EFC if the family:

1. Has an adjusted gross income equal to or less than the maximum income that may be earned to claim the maximum federal earned income tax credit, and

2. Does not and was not required to file an IRS Form 1040.

An example of the effect of this provision is as follows:

The income threshold for the maximum earned income tax credit was $11,850 for the 1991 tax year. The income threshold for the earned income tax credit is adjusted annually for inflation and was approximately $12,000 for the 1992 tax year. Thus, for the 1993-94 academic year, any student (other than an independent student without dependents) whose family's adjusted gross income is approximately $12,000 or less would automatically have a zero EFC.

INDEPENDENT STUDENT

Independent Student Definition

The definition of "independent student" has been revised to regard as independent any student who;

1. Is at least 24 years old by 12/31 of the award year;
2. Is an orphan or ward of the court;
3. Is a veteran of the Armed Forces of the United States;
4. Is a graduate or professional student;
5. Is a married student;
6. Is a spouse who has legal dependents other than a spouse; or
7. Is a student for whom a financial aid administrator determines and documents the student's independent status on the basis of unusual circumstances.

FINANCIAL AID ADMINISTRATOR DISCRETION

The HEA gives authority to a financial aid administrator (FAA) to make adjustments to a student's cost of attendance and EFC on the basis of an individual student's special circumstances rather than circumstances that exist across a class of students. Adjustments can either increase or decrease a student's EFC or cost of attendance. In the case of an adjustment to a student's EFC, the adjustment must relate to that student's special circumstances and must be documented in the student's file.

In addition, the HEA permits an FAA to request and use any supplementary information about the financial status or personal circumstances of a student or his or her family to determine whether special circumstances exist. The student or parent can not be charged a fee for the collection, processing, or delivery of such supplementary information.

If the student does not meet the above requirements for an independent student and the parents refuse to sign the financial aid application, there is really nothing the student can do. The student will not be eligible for governmental college aid, unless the FAA at the school will give you special dispensation. The student should consider cooperative education, a search of non-governmental loans or scholarships, or some other program.

A second year female student called requesting suggestions on what to do as her parents refused to sign the financial aid application. She informed me she had already switched from North Harris County

Community College to Prairie View A&M, a predominately black college. She had received a minority scholarship and had a part-time campus job, and was looking for other sources.

LOSS OF EMPLOYMENT BY APPLICANT

If the applicant worked full time (35 hours a week for at least 30 weeks) during the base year and is no longer employed full time, he or she may file under a special condition. This option is intended to help the applicant who leaves a job to go to school. (See the section above "Financial Aid Administrator Discretion".)

This condition is intended to accommodate independent students who reduce their hours of employment to go to school, but who still have a job. It includes situations where the student has been working two jobs and quits one to return to school. It also includes cases where the student has been fired or laid off, has retired or resigned, or has been on strike, on maternity leave, or on some other leave of absence.

When the student receives his/her financial aid report from the school, the student should take the report to his/her financial aid counselor and explain how her/his income has decreased from the base year reported on the form. With proper verification the counselor should adjust your financial aid assignment. The trouble is that by that time grants and low interest loans may be used up at the school. My suggestions are these. 1. Check with the financial aid office at your particular college to see how they would handle such a situation and what would be the time to quit your job to get the maximum aid benefit. Different colleges may give you different responses, so do what's best for you. 2. If the preceding doesn't allow you to make a clear-cut efficacious decision, check with a part time employer (like Manpower, Kelly, etc.) to see if you can keep body and soul together working through them after you quit your job. If so, before you quit your steady job, make up a reading list of books suggested by professors or your own desires, and do lots of reading when you quit your job. The list should include two books on memory techniques. They are quickly mastered and are very rewarding.

LOSS OF EMPLOYMENT BY SPOUSE

2 Start Early Filling In The Forms

If the independent applicant's spouse, whose income from work for the base year must be reported on the aid application, has lost his or her job for at least ten weeks in the current year, a special condition may be reported. Weeks of unemployment in the prior year (base year) should not be included in the ten-week period even if the weeks of unemployment were consecutive. For example, if the spouse lost his or her job December 1 of the base year, a special condition could not be reported until the second week of March, provided the spouse had been unemployed for the full ten week period after January 1.

This condition includes cases where the spouse has been fired or laid off, or has resigned or retired, or has been on strike, on maternity leave, or on some other leave of absence.

A LEGAL GUARDIAN OR AN ADOPTIVE PARENT

If a legal guardian is appointed by a court and is specifically required by the court to use his or her own financial resources to support the applicant then that applicant is considered dependent.

Sometimes the court order stipulates that such guardianship will stop when the child reaches a certain age. If the extant court order has such a condition, or the applicant knows at the time of application for school that the guardianship will cease before the applicant begins college or will cease in the course of the award year (before June 30, 1993 for 1993-94), the student should answer the questions about "parent" as if she or he had no legal guardian.

There is no necessity for credentials to support a student's claim that his or her guardian does not meet the definition of a guardian as outlined in the regulation. The aid administrator can rely upon such a claim by the applicant unless the school has different data.

When the student is adopted, the dependency questions are answered based upon the student's current legal relationship with the adoptive parents. If a student has applied as independent and is adopted during the award year, he/she must update dependency status. The new answers are based on the dependency questions as they apply to the adoptive parents (except on previously certified Stafford Loans [FFELPs]).

FOSTER PARENTS OR STEPPARENTS

Foster parents and stepparents who have neither adopted the applicant nor have been appointed legal guardians (as per the definition given above) for the applicant are not considered parents in determining a student's dependency status.

Living stepparents are not judged parents for the purpose of answering the dependency questions (unless the stepparent has legally adopted the applicant or been appointed legal guardian, as defined above). A stepparent who was married to a parent who is now deceased is not considered in answering the dependency questions. Unless the stepparent meets the definition of legal guardian or adoptive parent, the student applies as independent.

CHANGES IN DEPENDENCY STATUS

Suppose a student has answered the dependency questions inaccurately, or the student's status has changed. The student must refile the application. Suppose he or she has received a Pell Grant, SEOG or Perkins Loan, funds for which they no longer qualify. Then the student must repay these. Suppose the student files as an independent and collects the first disbursement, then discovers he/she is dependent. Then he/she must file a Correction Application for the Pell Grant. The financial aid officer must be notified of the change in dependency status for the SEOG and Perkins Loan. Then the student must comply with the school's method for amending or revising these awards.

Dependency condition may not be altered due to a change in marital status after the time of applying. The same condition pertains to the married student who properly files as independent but later divorces. The student is now single, but his or her dependency condition remains the same.

If a student makes an error in items concerning dependency status, but the error does not change the dependency status, on the application for financial aid all income and asset items should be scrutinized to make sure they reveal data for the correct person. If a student whose parents are divorced executes the application using the father's income because the father has claimed the student on his tax return, but the student actually lives with the mother, he or she should instead list the mother's income and assets. The student is dependent in either case. Incorrect data is on the application. Since dependency has not changed, the modifications are made directly on the SAR, not by filing a Correction

Corrections that change the applicant's dependency status must be made on a Correction Application. Changes in dependency status may not be made on the SAR.

REVERSING DEPENDENCY STATUS

Aid administrators were assigned by the Higher Education Amendments of 1986 the authority to favor students who have mistakenly identified themselves as dependent. Under these circumstances, the applicant should still respond freely to the dependency queries on the aid application as he/she interprets them. The financial aid officer will have the power to adjust his/her answers later if they are wrong.

MARITAL STATUS OF PARENTS OF DEPENDENTS

If the applicant's parents are divorced, then the marital status of the parent with whom the applicant lives is the correct answer to marital status, i.e., whether single or remarried. This same parent is the one whose financial data is used, no matter if this parent claims the student as a tax deduction or not.

PARENTS DIVORCED OR SEPARATED

Family data on applications refer to the parent responsible for the student. This is not necessarily the parent who claims the student on his/her tax return. The parent with whom the student lived the most during the past 12 months is that parent. If the student lived with neither parent, or lived with each parent an equal number of days, the parent who provided the greater amount of support in the past 12 months is the parent listed.

STEPPARENTS

Starting with 88-89 academic year, a dependent student must include data for a stepparent who currently is married to the parent he/she specifies on the form.

No exceptions to this rule are allowed. Denial of support from the stepparent is unacceptable. For all items on the application besides the dependency questions, the term "parents" includes the stepparent; the stepparent's income and assets must be given. You will remember from an earlier paragraph that if the parent, the spouse of the step-parent, dies, then the step-parent is not considered a parent.

SPOUSE OF A LEGAL GUARDIAN

A legal guardian's spouse is considered a step-parent. The income and assets of the guardian's spouse must be reported only if legal guardianship is continuing throughout the award year and if the guardian was married at the time of application.

STATE OF LEGAL RESIDENCE OF PARENTS

The state of legal residence of the parents is normally the same as that of the dependent applicant, but this is not necessarily true. An applicant with married parents residing in two different states is the legal resident of the state of the parent with whom the applicant resides. For parents living outside the United States, the state where they are registered to vote, own property, or pay taxes is their residence. A parent serving with the Armed Forces is a resident of the state in which the parent resided when inducted into the armed service.

INDEPENDENT APPLICANT

Household size for an independent applicant includes: 1-the applicant; 2-the applicant's spouse; 3-the applicant's dependent children i.e., children receiving half or more of their support from the applicant; 4-other persons who, at the time of application, live with and receive half or more of their support from the applicant and spouse and will keep getting this assistance for the award year between July 1 and June 30. Household size may also include an unborn child.

With the definition of an independent student in the Higher Education Amendments of 1986 and the Technical Amendments of 1987, a child attending college may be considered independent for Title IV aid, but still be part of the parent's household. If the student is 24 or older, he or she is considered independent for Title IV funds. He or she may still be deemed dependent for the parent's taxes.

FOSTER CHILDREN

Foster children are not technically dependents of the foster parents. Normally, foster parents do not contribute more than 50% of their support. Hence, they are not included in the household size for financial aid application purposes. However, they may be counted in the household size, if the foster children qualify as "other persons", that is if they are dependents on the foster parents' tax form.

UNBORN CHILD

If the applicant or parent of a dependent applicant has a baby in the award year, he or she is included in the parents' household size, if and only if the parent provides more than half the child's support from birth until the end of the award year. The same is true for the independent student in an expectant situation. As the above information makes clear, all financial aid applications must be updated for household size.

INCOME TAX RETURN EXEMPTIONS

The reason the number of exemptions recorded on the U.S. income tax return is recorded on the aid application is that it will be used to compare the reported AGI and U.S. tax paid.

The number of exemptions and the number in the household may or may not agree as recounted on the financial aid form. Persons other than those living in the household may be listed if the filer contributes more than 50 percent of their support, i.e. a grandparent living in a nursing home, etc. The size of the household recorded on the student aid form may also show changes in the family not shown in the number of tax exemptions which are caused by births, deaths, etc.

HOUSEHOLD SIZE AND THE DEPENDENT APPLICANT

The total number of people the applicant's parents will support during the award year (July 1 through June 30) for which the application is made is the size of the parents' household . The number includes parents or stepparent, if appropriate, the applying student, the other children who get more than half their support from the parents, other children who attend post-secondary schools at least half time and qualify for purposes of Title IV aid as dependent, are considered part of the parents' household.

It is possible for a college student, considered independent for Title IV purposes to also be part of a dependent applicant's household size. That is, if the student is at least 24 years of age, he or she is judged independent for Title IV purposes, even if he or she still receives more than half their support from the parents. The student may still be included in the parents' household on the dependent applicant's application, because the definition of "dependents of the parent" does not exclude such a possibility.

Part of the parents' household is also 1) those who live with and receive half or more of their support from the applicant's parents when applying and will continue to receive this support during the award year; 2) stepchildren are part of the household size when treated as the applicant's siblings, or when they meet the definition of "other children" for purposes of household size as explained in the first paragraph of this section.

If the dependent applicant is married and if he or she meets the definition of "other children", then the applicant's spouse should be included in the total size of the parents' household. Also an unborn child awaited in the award year by spouse or applicant is counted as a member of the household.

If the student applicant is not included in the family size, this is an error. The error is corrected for the Pell Grant by making the change to the appropriate item on the SAR. For college funds, the applicant reports the error to the financial aid officer and follow the college's method for correcting the data.

INDEPENDENT APPLICANT AND HOUSEHOLD SIZE

An independent applicant's household size contains the applicant, the applicant's spouse, the applicant's dependent children for whom they provide at least half support, and an unborn child may be included in household size, see above. Furthermore, as with household size for the Pell Grant, the number of family members in college must be updated when the student submits the SAR to the college. If the application is selected for confirmation, the number must be updated at the time of confirmation.

Once submission and/or verification has taken place if required, this number may not be changed for Pell Grant resolution. However, for campus-based funds, the college has the option of requiring updated facts throughout the award year. This need to update is true of dependent students also.

PARENTS SEPARATED OR DIVORCED

Since the aid application requires only one parent's income to be reported in cases of divorce or separation, an applicant may file a special condition only if his or her parents have separated or divorced after filing the original application.

If the separation or divorce is between a parent and a stepparent, the stepparent's income must have been required to be reported on the previous application for the change to allow filing under a special condition.

If the separation or divorce occurred prior to filing the original application, the applicant should have reported only the data of the custodial parent. If the income and assets of both parents were reported, the SAR should be corrected rather than reporting a special condition, and the student and parent should inform the aid administrator of the error.

DEATH OF A PARENT

If a parent or stepparent whose base year income must be reported dies after the submission of an earlier application, the applicant may file under a special condition. However, if the parent referred to was the last surviving parent with whom the applicant had a dependency relationship, the applicant must file under the special condition as an independent student if he or she wishes to use income for the projected year. In this case, only the student's income is used to calculate Pell Grant eligibility.

Even if the applicant continues to live with a stepparent after the financially responsible natural parent dies, the applicant is still considered independent unless the stepparent has legally adopted the applicant or has legal obligations under a court-ordered guardianship to support the applicant from his or her own resources.

The purpose of the special condition is to reflect a change in income under certain conditions. If a parent of a dependent applicant dies but had no income during the base year, a special condition does not apply.

If the death occurred prior to filing any application, a regular application should have been used, reporting only the income of the surviving parent. If a regular application was filed, but both incomes were reported, the aid administrator for the campus-based and Stafford Loan programs must be told, and corrections must be made on the SAR for Pell Grant. If the last parent died before the student filed any application, the student should have filed the original application as an independent; if he/she did not, a Correction Application should be filed.

3 SPECIAL CONDITIONS FOR INDEPENDENT STUDENTS

SEPARATION OR DIVORCE

If the applicant and his or her spouse separate or divorce after the applicant has already applied for a Pell Grant, a special condition may be reported. If no application has been filed, the student should use a regular application, excluding the spouse's income and assets. If the student filed a regular application after the separation or divorce occurred but reported the information of the spouse, the corrections should be made on the SAR and reported to the aid administrator.

DEATH OF A SPOUSE

An independent applicant may file under a special condition if his or her spouse dies after a regular aid application for Pell Grant has been filed. As in the case of separation or divorce, if no aid application has been filed, a regular application should be used, excluding the information of the spouse. If the regular application was filed after the death and the student gave spouse's information, corrections are made on the SAR and should also be reported to the aid administrator.

DEATH OF THE LAST SURVIVING PARENT OF A DEPENDENT STUDENT

A previously dependent student may file under a special condition using his/her estimated financial information if the last surviving parent with whom he/she had a dependency relationship dies after a regular application has been filed. If the death occurred before any application had been filed, the student should have met the definition of independent and should have filed as such.

SPECIAL CONDITION AND SIMPLIFIED NEEDS TEST

Base year income is used to determine the student's eligibility to use the simplified need analysis formula. If the student meets the special condition qualifications, then the simplified formula is applied, using current year information. "The calculation of family contribution for all Title IV programs shall be based on a simplified formula for families that have adjusted gross incomes equal to or less than $12,000, and who are

3 Special Conditions for Independent Students

not required to file a Federal Income Tax return, or, if they are required to file, file either an IRS tax return form 1040A or 1040EZ.

Since the family must qualify as a unit for the simplified need analysis, all family members whose income must be reported on the aid income application must be counted in determining the $12,000 limit. If any member whose income must be counted filed an IRS 1040 (i.e., the long form as opposed to a 1040A or 1040EZ), the simplified analysis may not be used. In the case of a dependent student whose family meets these requirements, both the parental contribution and the student contribution components of the EFC are calculated using the simplified analysis.

There are six elements to be used: adjusted gross income; federal taxes paid; an allowance for state and other taxes; untaxed income and other benefits; number of family members; number of family members in post-secondary education.

Because many of the elements of the regular formula are not used in this analysis, the simplified need formula is regarded as the "short" formula. The simplified need analysis is always performed using base year income.

CORRECTION APPLICATION

As noted the Correction Application is used only to correct or change dependency status or report a special condition. The Correction Application is simply a regular ASFA with "Correction Application" printed on top; however, a regular application with "Correction" written on it may not be used for this purpose.

Since there are no special instructions that accompany the Correction Application, the student may require more help in completing it. There are five situations for which a Correction Application may need to be filed:

1) correction of dependency status that was reported erroneously on the original application

2) updating dependency status when it changes (for reasons other than

3 Special Conditions for Independent Students

a change in marital status) after filing the original application

3) cases where, under the new independent student definition the aid administrator makes a documented decision that a student who does not meet one of the other provisions of the definition is, in fact, independent

4) cases where a student otherwise qualifies as independent but cannot be treated as such because he or she was treated as independent in the previous award year and was claimed as a dependent by anyone other than a spouse for the first calendar year of that award year

5) cases where a student (or student's spouse or dependent student's parent) qualifies for one of the special conditions for which the student can not initially apply.

Updating is required whenever a change in dependency occurs, except for previously certified Stafford (FFELP) applications. In any case, marital status may not be updated unless the student qualifies for a special condition in which the student has separated, divorced or become widowed. If the student filed the original application as "single", the Correction Application must also indicate "single" even if the student has married since the time of original filing. The fact that all information is to be reported as it should have been when the original application was filed (except for updating of the dependency questions) may be a source of confusion to the student.

4 INCOME

VETERANS EDUCATIONAL BENEFITS

Only the student's own VA educational benefits should be included here. Spouse VA benefits are no longer reported on this part of the form.

Death Pension Benefits and Dependency Indemnity Compensation (DIC) should not be included in this item; they are included elsewhere. It should be noted, however, that at age 18, a DIC recipient has the option of converting to DEA (Dependents Educational Assistance) benefits.

The amount the applicant expects to receive per month from veterans G.I. Bill and Dependents Educational Assistance benefits are reported in one entry; the corresponding number of months within the award year he or she will be eligible is also reported.

The amount per month and number of months the applicant will receive veterans VA Contributory Benefits are reported separately. Both the student's and the government's portions must be included.

OTHER AWARD YEAR INCOME

The applicant, whether dependent or independent, and spouse are asked to estimate their income separately.

FOREIGN INCOME

If an applicant's or parent's income is from a foreign country and is filed in an income tax return with a central government outside the U.S., the information from that form should be used to complete the aid application. All figures should be expressed in U.S. dollars using the conversion rate in effect on the day the application is being completed.

This income must be reported on the aid application even if the laws of the foreign country prohibit the earner from removing the income from that country.

The income is reported as untaxed income if no income tax was paid to

4 Income

a central government (foreign or U.S.). Any amount excluded on a U.S. tax return (foreign income exclusion) is reported as untaxed income. However, if both U.S. and foreign tax returns are filed and the only amount appearing on the U.S. return is the foreign income exclusion, only the foreign tax return should be used.

NO TAX RETURN WILL BE FILED

The inquiries pertaining to income from the tax return are skipped if the filer was exempt from filing a U.S. income tax return. Only the income data below will be reported on the financial aid application:

1) Income earned from work by the parents and/or by the applicant and spouse. This includes earnings from W-2 forms as well as earnings from other work not included on a W-2 form, such as farm or business income 2) Social Security benefits received 3) Aid to Families with Dependent Children (AFDC or ADC) benefits received 4) Child support collected 5) Other untaxed income and benefits collected. This includes interest and dividend income.

Total income is determined by adding together the entries for the items listed above.

USING ESTIMATED INCOME DATA

If a return has not yet been filed, the answers to the questions on the application must approximate as closely as possible those that will be on the tax return when it is filed. The applicant or parents should use a blank income tax form and actual W-2 forms or other documents to insure the estimates are as accurate as possible. Estimated information must correspond to the information eventually entered on the tax form and submitted to the IRS.

If it does not, the applicant must correct the SAR so that figures do correspond to comparable items on the tax form and inform the financial aid office of any discrepancies. Since there are tolerances allowed the applicant should consult the aid administrator to determine whether the corrections are actually necessary. Income figures are subject to verification once the institution receives a copy of the IRS 1040, 1040A, or 1040EZ.

Unless an institution has in its files conflicting information regarding a student's financial situation, or unless the applicant is required to be verified, the institution may rely on the information provided by the student in determining his or her need. Thus, if a student files a financial aid application using estimated data, there is no institutional liability if aid is awarded using the resulting need analysis unless the institution has information showing discrepancies. In such a case, the application must be verified. That is, the institution must require the student to provide documentation necessary to verify the information and/or resolve any discrepancies. The institution may require any applicant whose income was estimated to verify that information, if the student has not already been selected for verification by the processor.

EXPECTED INCOME EARNED FROM WORK

The applicant must estimate his or her earnings, other than earnings from need-based financial aid programs, for the current year. The applicant's spouse's earnings must also be estimated and entered into the appropriate place on the aid application. For the dependent student, the mother's and father's estimated current year earnings are also to be given, each as a separate entry. Income expected to be earned by a parent who is also a student should not include need-based student financial aid.

Earnings are collected separately from other expected income, because the need analysis formulas include an additional allowance for households where both parents (or for independent students, both the student and spouse) work, or where there is a single parent who works.

INCOME REPORTING ON TAX FORMS

If the applicant is divorced, separated, or widowed, information for the spouse should not be included. If the applicant is married when applying, he or she must include the income of the spouse.

In the case of an applicant and spouse, or the parents of a dependent applicant who file separately but are married and living together, data

4 Income

from both returns must be combined on the aid application.

If a couple lives together, the aid administrator can inquire as to the State's definition of common law marriage.

FISCAL YEAR TAX RETURNS

If a tax return is filed based on a fiscal year rather than a calendar year, the fiscal year which contains the most months of the base year is used in completing the aid application. If the fiscal year ends June 30, the return which includes the first half of the base year must be used, so that an equal number of months of the base year is included on two fiscal year returns.

EXCLUSIONS TO INCOME OF NATIVE AMERICANS

AMERICAN INDIAN CLAIMS ACTS

Under the ALASKA NATIVE CLAIMS SETTLEMENT ACT (ANCSA) OR THE MAINE INDIAN CLAIMS SETTLEMENT ACT any moneys obtained should be excluded by Native Americans from their income. Payments of $2,000 or less obtained from the PER CAPITA ACT OR THE DISTRIBUTION OF JUDGMENT FUNDS ACT are also excluded. Just the amount over $2,000 per disbursement obtained under these two acts in the base year should be reported as income. Recognize that the $2,000 exclusion applies on a PER PAYMENT BASIS, not on the total received for the year. For instance if ten separate $2,000 payments were obtained, none of that income need be reported. But for one payment of $20,000, the recipient would have to report $18,000 as income.

Regarding ANCSA, only that income which ensues directly from the Act may be excluded. For instance, funds obtained from sale of land parceled out as a compensation from the Act would not be reported. Stock dividends resulting from corporate profits, however, are not excepted, and so would be reported.

INCOME EARNED FROM WORK FOR BASE YEAR

This figure includes all wages, salaries, tips, and commissions, with the exception of need-based financial aid (such as College Work-Study and need-based Cooperative Education Program earnings.) Income earned from work also includes business and farm income.

The earnings of each parent are shown separately, as are the earnings of the applicant and his or her spouse.

INCOME FROM FINANCIAL AID AWARDS

Student financial aid covers scholarships, loans, grants, and need-based employment. These awards should be excluded from adjusted gross income, income earned from work, untaxed income, and estimated income on the financial aid form. No U. S. income tax should be paid on these amounts on these forms. This applies to independent applicants, dependent applicants, and parents of dependent applicants, if the parents are students themselves and received financial aid.

CORRECTIONS TO ESTIMATED INCOME

A student may correct his or her application if there is an error in the original estimate of "expected income" (for example, the inclusion of FWS earnings in error) but may not correct this item if the original estimate was sound at the time of application.

For example, updating the "expected income" to reflect a change in circumstances such as loss of employment would not be sufficient reason to correct the information originally given on the application.

VA benefits are subject to verification under the General Provisions requirement to resolve conflicting data. Once verified, however, the amount of benefits reported do not need to be updated, even if the VA law changes during the award year.

A significant change in income should always be reported to the financial aid officer.

JOBS IN COOPERATIVE EDUCATION

A cooperative education job is considered to be student financial aid if

4 Income

it is awarded on the basis of need and is considered part of the financial aid package. The co-op terms must be required by the institution, or be part of the structure of an elected course of study in order to qualify the earnings as financial aid. As financial aid, it should not be reported as "income" on the financial aid application.

5 Other Income

5 OTHER INCOME

TYPES OF INCOME AND BENEFITS TO BE INCLUDED IN "OTHER UNTAXED INCOME AND BENEFITS"

Forms of untaxed income that do not show on a tax return and which must be included in the entry for "other untaxed income and benefits" include:

1. Payments to tax-deferred pension and savings plans (paid directly or withheld form earnings), including the 401K and 403b plans;

2. Welfare benefits (except AFDC or ADC, which are reported separately);

3. Worker's Compensation;

4. Non-educational Veterans benefits such as Death Pension, Dependency and Indemnity Compensation, etc. are untaxed income and should be included in all non-educational VA benefits received by the applicant or by the parents of a dependent applicant on behalf of all family members. Educational benefits and VA Vocational Rehabilitation benefits for post-secondary education should not be included.

5. Housing, food, and other living allowances, except rent subsidies for low-income housing, for military, clergy, and others (both cash payments and cash value of benefits), should be included.

NOTE: Military personnel and clergy are often given a housing allowance or free housing as a supplement to their salaries. Living and housing allowances must be reported if these allowances are a form of compensation. Utilities are not considered in calculating untaxed income. For example, if a minister owns his or her house but the mortgage payments and the utilities are paid by the church, only the total mortgage payments made by the church on the minister's behalf during the base year should be considered in calculating untaxed income.

6. Cash support or any money paid on the parents' or student's behalf;

7. In situations where the parents' or student's monetary obligations

5 Other Income

(such as mortgage payments or rent, car payments, utilities, tuition, etc.) are paid by a friend or relative the value of these payments must be reported as untaxed income.

However, this requirement does not apply to a student who is being provided free board and room by a relative (not a parent) or other person. Only payment of an actual monetary obligation is untaxed income. For example, if a student rents an apartment and the rent is paid by a friend or relative (or parent in the case of an independent student), those payments are untaxed income.

8. Black Lung benefits;

9. Refugee Assistance;

10. Untaxed portions of Railroad Retirement Benefits;

11. Job Training Partnership Act non-educational benefits:

Generally JTPA benefits are educational benefits because the beneficiary is a student. However, when the person is no longer a student, JTPA funds may be used to pay part of a person's salary during probationary on-the-job training, under some circumstances. If a dependent student's parents or the applicant receives JTPA funds, but is not enrolled as a student (non-educational JTPA benefits), the applicant is instructed to report these benefits as other untaxed income of the parent or independent applicant, or as the dependent applicant's untaxed income.

12. Any other untaxed income and benefits which do not appear on a tax return.

Untaxed income or benefits which appear on a tax return are to be included as part of the entry for "other untaxed income and benefits" only if they were not already reported elsewhere on the application as separate entries. These forms of untaxed income include:

DEDUCTIBLE IRA AND KEOGH PAYMENTS

NOTE: Due to changes brought about by the Tax Reform Act of 1986,

5 Other Income

payments to IRA and Keogh Plans are not always fully deductible beginning with the 1987 tax filing year. Part of these payments may, therefore, be included in adjusted gross income. Any deductible portions are to be reported as other untaxed income.

Prior to 1988-89, these deductions were not considered part of income in the Pell Grant methodology; they were, however, under Uniform Methodology. Therefore, aid applications for 1987-88 and earlier collected information on IRA and Keogh Plan deductions as a separate data element. Beginning with 1988-89, such deductions are considered discretionary uses of relative income and are treated as untaxed income in both the Congressional and Pell Grant methodologies.

Earned income credits are:

Untaxed portions of pensions (excluding "rollovers");

Credit for federal tax on special fuels (non-farmers only; for farmers, this source of income is part of adjusted gross income and should not be double-counted by including it as untaxed income);

Foreign income exclusion;

Tax exempt interest income.

MORE ABOUT UNTAXED INCOME

The aid administrator may run into other forms of untaxed income for the base year, the current year, or the award year which require some additional explanation. For example ROTC stipends received for periods of non-enrollment only (such as amounts received during summer months) are included as untaxed income. Resident assistant-ship benefits (free room and board, for example) should be included under untaxed income if the resident assistant-ship was not awarded as financial aid; these benefits fall under "housing, food, and other living allowances".

Money received by a dependent applicant from the non-custodial parent when the parents are divorced or separated is included as untaxed

5 Other Income

income of the applicant. Not to be included as the applicant's income are child support payments paid to the custodial parent. These payments are included under the parent's untaxed income. If the non-custodial parent pays a monetary obligation of the applicant (such as tuition), the amount paid is reported as untaxed income of the applicant. Note that in the latter situation the parent is making payment directly to the person or institution holding the obligation (such as the school in the case of tuition).

Foster care money received for foster children is **not** reported as untaxed income, even though the foster child may meet the definition of "other person" under household size. If the foster child is an applicant for aid, support payments made by a court to a parent or to the foster parents are **not** reported as income.

Insurance settlements may or may not be counted as income, depending on the situation. Reimbursements for loss of an asset (such as a stolen car) or reimbursement for medical bills from injuries are **not** reported as income. However, portions of settlements received over and above these reimbursements are considered income and must be reported. If this income is not taxable, it will be included on the application as untaxed income.

6 COMPUTATION OF TAXES ON FORMS

AMOUNT OF U.S. INCOME TAX PAID

The actual amount of U.S. income tax paid is entered, not necessarily the amount shown on the W-2 form. FICA, self-employment tax, and other taxes should not be included in "U.S. income tax paid," 2nor should taxes paid on student financial aid.

When no tax return is filed, this question on the application is disregarded. If no tax return will be filed, tax withheld is not entered as tax paid. It is left blank.

JOINT RETURN FOR SEPARATED, ETC. PARENT OR APPLICANT

If you are a separated, divorced, or widowed parent or applicant who has filed a joint tax return with a former spouse, there are two methods of computing your share of income tax paid. 1) Determining what proportion of the AGI you were responsible for, then applying that percentage to the tax paid. 2) Using the IRS tax table to figure the amount of income tax you would have paid if a separate return had been filed.

MARRIED COUPLE FILES SEPARATE RETURNS

If the applicant and spouse, or the parents of a dependent applicant, are married and living together but filed separately, the information from both returns must be combined and entered together on the aid application.

In situations where a couple lives together, the aid administrator may wish to inquire as to the State's definition of common law marriage.

7 FINISHING THE APPLICATION FORM

WHO GETS THE MDE ANALYSIS

The application forms used by the MDE processing services do not include the question concerning defaults or owed refunds, but ask the applicant instead to list the names, addresses, and code numbers of all the institutions, agencies, or programs that are to receive copies of the financial aid and need analysis reports.

If, after filing the application, the applicant wishes to add one or more colleges not listed on the original, this may be done by filling out a form sent to the applicant as part of the service's acknowledgement or receipt of the application form.

CERTIFICATION AND SIGNATURES

The student applicant is required to sign the application form. In addition, a dependent student's application must be signed by at least one parent, and a married student's application must be signed by his or her spouse. Each person signing the form is certifying that all information on the form is correct and that he or she is willing to provide documents (including a copy of the U.S. income tax return) to verify the information provided.

An application for federal funds will not be processed if the application is signed prior to January 1. This now applies to the MDE processing services as well as to the federal processor.

PARENT'S SIGNATURE NOT AVAILABLE

Under certain specific conditions, a third party (for example, a guidance counselor) may sign the application in place of the parent of a dependent student. This is permissible only if:

the parent(s) is not currently in the United States and cannot be contacted by normal means of communication;
the current address of the parent(s) is not known; or the parent(s) has been determined physically or mentally incapable of providing a

signature.

The signature of the counselor or financial aid administrator serves as a mechanism to get the application through the processing system and also assures a minimum level of creditability in the data submitted. However, the counselor or administrator does not assume any responsibility or liability in this process. If the financial aid office finds any inaccuracies in the information reported, the student should be directed to make corrections through the normal process.

SPOUSE'S SIGNATURE REQUIRED

As stated above, the married applicant's spouse as well as the applicant must sign the application form, certifying that all of the information on the application is correct and that, if required, he or she is willing to give documents such as an income tax return to prove that the information is correct. Under certain circumstances, in the process of verifying the information on the application, the spouse's signature on documents used for verification may be waived. The spouse's signature is not required if the spouse can't be located because of an unknown address, the spouse is deceased, mentally or physically incapacitated, or is residing in a country other than the U.S. and can't be reached by normal means of communication.

PROCESSING THE APPLICATION FORM

Whether filing the federal application form or an MDE form applicants should not enclose any additional materials such as explanatory letters, work-sheets, tax forms, etc. Any such materials enclosed with the application will be destroyed by shredding--no material will be returned to the applicant. Such materials, if requested, should be sent directly to the aid administrator by the applicant.

To insure against loss in mailing or processing, the applicant should **always** retain a copy of the application. This is useful if questions arise during processing regarding any information submitted on the form or if the application is selected for verification.

NAME AND ADDRESS OF DESIRED COLLEGE

7 Finishing the Application Form

The federal application form (AFSA) requests the applicant to indicate the name and complete mailing address of the institution he or she plans to attend (including the branch if it is a multi-campus institution). The applicant is instructed to leave this question blank if he or she is undecided.

Information from this question is used by the central processor to prepare lists of applicants who indicate they are planning to attend a given institution.

The Pell Grant report (SAR) is mailed directly to the student applicant. The financial aid office does not receive a copy of the SAR unless it is submitted to the institution by the student.

If the applicant indicates the name of a college on the AFSA, then decides to attend a different college, it is not necessary to notify the federal processing service. However, if the applicant has submitted his or her SAR to one institution then decides to transfer to another eligible institution, the applicant must obtain a duplicate SAR from the federal processor. The student may not file a new application.

APPLICATION FOR FEDERAL STUDENT AID (AFSA)

A mailing envelope is provided with the application form and should be used. The AFSA instructions provide an address for inquiries if the student does not receive a SAR in four weeks. The same address is used to request duplicate SARs.

7 Finishing the Application Form

INSTITUTIONAL FEES

The Higher Education Amendments of 1986 prohibit the institution from charging any student or parent of a student a fee for processing or handling any application, form, or data required to determine the student's eligibility for Title IV student assistance, or the amount of such assistance. A student or parent may be charged a fee for processing an institutional or State financial aid form or elements not required by the Secretary.

8 Corrections to Application Data

8 CORRECTIONS TO APPLICATION DATA

TYPES OF CORRECTIONS

There are a number of instances when it is necessary to make corrections or revisions to information originally submitted. There are also different methods of reporting the changes, depending on the type of change and/or aid program involved. The following paragraphs cover the types of changes.

CLERICAL OR ARITHMETIC ERROR

If the applicant believes a clerical or arithmetic error has occurred, an applicant may request a re-computation of his or her expected family contribution. The procedure for doing so is provided on the SAR.

ERRORS IN INFORMATION PROVIDED

If the information submitted was inaccurate when the application was signed, corrections must be made unless the aid administrator determines that such corrections fall within allowable tolerances.

ITEMS SUBJECT TO UPDATING

Updating occurs when the answer to an application item was correct at the time of application, but has changed since the application has been filed. If items are subject to updating, such changes must be reported. Items not specifically subject to updating may not be changed to reflect new information. There are three items that are required to be updated, if changes occur after completion of the application and under certain circumstances:

Dependency must be updated for all programs except previously certified Stafford Loans (FFELPs), whenever a change occurs, unless the change results from a change in marital status. Changes resulting from a change in marital status may not be made.

Household Size and Number of Family Members Attending Post-secondary Institutions are also sometimes subject to updating. For these

8 Corrections to Application Data

two items, updating requirements depend on whether or not the student is selected for verification. If selected, the student must update both items to be accurate as of the time of verification (as defined by the institution). For Pell Grant, updating may not occur once verification has taken place. If not subject to verification for Pell Grant, these items must be updated so they are correct as of the date the student submits his/her first SAR to the institution.

It should be noted that these are the only items which may be updated. Data items such as assets and projected income may not be updated if changes occur after filing; such data may be changed only if errors were made in the original reporting of those values. Marital status or changes in other items due to a change in marital status may not be updated. Of course, for the campus-based and Stafford Loan programs only, the aid administrator may exercise his or her professional judgment to assess the reasonableness of the family contribution in light of unusual or new circumstances. Any changes made to an EFC must be documented.

CORRECTIONS MADE AFTER DISBURSEMENT OF FUNDS

If a disbursement of federal funds has been made on the basis of the original application, and if items subject to updating are then changed or errors are corrected, the student is required to repay any portion of federal funds already received for which, on the basis of the corrected application, the student is no longer eligible. If the over-award can be rectified by adjusting subsequent disbursements for that award year, then repayment is not necessary.

9 THE MOST USED AWARDS

FEDERAL PELL GRANT PROGRAM

The HEA Amendment of 1992 has renamed the program from the "Pell Grant Program" to the "Federal Pell Grant Program."

DETERMINATION OF NEED

The amended statute deletes the Pell Grant Program family contribution schedule. The law now requires that an applicant's expected family contribution (EFC) and cost of attendance for the Federal Pell Grant Program be determined under the requirements of Need Analysis.

MINIMUM AWARD

The amended law increases the minimum Federal Pell Grant award from $200 to $400. However, a student who qualifies for an award equal to or greater than $200 but less than $400 automatically receives a $400 award.

MAXIMUM AWARD

The statute sets the maximum authorized Federal Pell Grant award at $3,700 for the 1993-94 award year and provides for $200 increases per year for the next 4 years. (Under the fiscal year 1993 appropriations act the amount of the actual maximum award will be $2,300 for the 1993-94 award year.) A student's award is the lesser of the following three amounts: (1) The maximum award minus the expected family contribution; or (2) The cost of attendance minus the expected family contribution; or (3) When an appropriations act provides a maximum award amount exceeding $2,400, the sum of: (a) $2,400; and (b) one-half of the difference between $2,400 and the maximum award; and (c) the lesser of (i) the remaining one-half of the difference in (b); or (ii) the sum of the student's tuition and, if the student has dependent-care expenses or disability-related expenses, a $750 allowance.

INSUFFICIENT APPROPRIATIONS

The new statute deletes the "linear reduction" formula that was used to adjust awards downward when the funds available were insufficient to make full awards. The new provision requires the Secretary to notify Congress of any funding shortfall and the amount needed to be appropriated to fund the program fully at the maximum award level set in that fiscal year's appropriations language.

LESS THAN HALF-TIME ELIGIBILITY

Students who are enrolled at institutions of higher education on less than a half-time basis who otherwise meet eligibility criteria are now eligible to receive a Federal Pell Grant award.

OUTPUT DOCUMENT

A financial aid administrator at an institution of higher education shall use a student's EFC and the data used to calculate the EFC provided by the application central processing system (CPS) contractor on its regular output documents to the institution as well as the student's federal Student Aid Report (SAR) to make a Federal Pell Grant award. If there is a change in the student's data, the institution recalculates the student's EFC and makes the student's Federal Pell award in the correct amount. The corrected information must be reported on Part 2 of the student's SAR.

DURATION OF ELIGIBILITY

The statute eliminates the limits on the number of years that a student may receive Federal Pell Grants. This change applies to all students including students who had received the maximum number of grants under the current limitations that are applicable through the 1992-93 Award Year. The statute now permits eligible students, starting in the 1993-94 Award Year, to receive Federal Pell Grants during the time necessary to complete the student's first baccalaureate degree.

TWO FEDERAL PELL GRANTS IN A 12-MONTH PERIOD

The statute provides that the Secretary may allow, on a case-by-case basis, a student to receive two Federal Pell Grants during a single 12-month period if (1) the student is enrolled full-time in a baccalaureate program of at least 2 years at an institution of higher education that computes enrollment in credit hours; and (2) the student completes course work toward completion of a bachelor's degree that exceeds the requirements for a full academic year as defined by the institution.

INCARCERATED STUDENTS

The statute provides that in general an incarcerated student may receive a Federal Pell Grant. The amount of the incarcerated student's Federal Pell Grant may not exceed the cost of the tuition and fees normally assessed by the institution of higher education for that course of study, plus an allowance for books and supplies. An incarcerated student may not receive a Federal Pell Grant if he or she is serving under sentence of death or under a life sentence without the possibility of parole. Federal Pell Grants shall only be awarded to individuals who are incarcerated in a state that uses the Federal Pell Grants to supplement, and not to supplant, the level of postsecondary educational assistance provided by the state to incarcerated students in fiscal year 1988.

STUDY ABROAD

The amended statute provides for the payment of a Federal Pell Grant to a student who is participating in a program of study abroad that is approved for credit by the institution of higher education at which the student is enrolled. The new wording also permits making use of the foreign institutions costs when those costs exceed the cost of attendance at the student's home institution and the home institution's financial aid administrator deems those costs to be reasonable.

PELL GRANT PROGRAM

For each award year, application filing deadlines are established by the Department of Education. The current deadline is May 1 of the award year (May 1, 1993 for the award year 1993-94). The application must be received by the processor by that date.

The federal processor must receive the Correction Application or corrections to an applicant's Student Aid Report by July 30 of the award year. This date already takes into account extensions for submitting a

9 The Most Used Awards

SAR selected for verification; there is no additional extension for applications requiring verification. It should be noted, however, that a student must submit a first SAR with a calculated index by June 30 or the student's last day of enrollment, whichever comes first. For SARs requiring verification, there is a 60-day extension to submit a corrected SAR, if the first (June 30) deadline was met. The deadline for submitting corrections via either the SAR or the Correction Application is July 30 to allow sufficient time for processing and for the student to get the corrected SAR to the school by the extended deadline.

Pell Grants are awarded to students who need money for education after high school. A Pell Grant is not a loan; therefore, it does not have to be repaid. To get a Pell Grant a student must be an undergraduate without a bachelor's degree. To get a Pell Grant a student must go to school at least half-time. As the family contribution decreases the grant should increase.

Over one million applications will be selected for validation. That means the applicant must submit copies of income tax forms and other documents. Applications selected for validation are usually selected because some figures on the form are not in the range of predetermined criteria.

Almost one third of all applicants receive a rejection edit. This means some correction or verification is required. Applicants most likely to be rejected are those leaving critical fields blank, those reporting zero income or non-taxable income greater than $12,499, those listing marital status as widowed but showing two incomes, those having high unusual expenses, and those with farm assets under $1,000.

Whenever a drastic change in your personal or financial circumstances occurs after completing your application, request a Special Condition Application from your Financial Aid Officer, and submit it to the FAO as soon as feasible.

The amount of your award depends on your Student Aid Index number, the cost of the school, whether you are a full time or part time student, and whether you are going for a full academic year or less. If you are a half time student, your award will be one half.

The school will credit the money to your account, pay you directly, or a combination of both. If for some reason the school is late in crediting or paying you this award, they will debit school costs (tuition, etc.) against this account.

ALLOCATIONS FOR SENIORS

The college will not make disbursements to seniors on the basis of full-time enrollment, for less than 12 credit hours, even though the senior needs less than 12 credits to graduate,

PELL GRANTS NOT AWARDED ON PROBATIONARY ADMITTANCE

Admittance to a college on a probationary basis to ascertain if the student can perform on a college level does not allow the student to apply the hours taken to a certificate/degree, and therefore he/she can not receive Pell Grant assistance for those hours.

FINANCIAL AID TRANSCRIPT REQUIRED

If a student enrolls in another institution but has attended one or more formerly, the student must submit a financial aid transcript from the other institution(s) the student has attended. If there was any financial aid received, the transcript will provide information on that received.

GRADUATE LEVEL COURSES TAKEN BY UNDERGRADUATE

If graduate level courses that count toward their undergraduate degree are enrolled in by an undergraduate, then these courses can be counted in that student's enrollment status.

ENROLLMENT IN HIGH SCHOOL AND COLLEGE

A student enrolled in a secondary school at the same time as college is automatically ineligible for Title IV Aid. This applies to the intellectually gifted.

COMBINED DEGREE PROGRAMS, UNDERGRADUATE/GRADUATE

A program, resulting in an undergraduate and graduate degree, allows the student eligibility for consideration in the Pell Grant for the first four years. If a student transfers, after completing three years of undergraduate study into such a program, then the student is eligible for one more year only.

VETERINARY MEDICINE

A student, admitted into a veterinary program before finishing the undergraduate program, is eligible for the Pell Grant only in the first two years of required college work and the first two years of the veterinary program. Thereafter the student is not classified as an undergraduate, and is ineligible for the Pell Grant.

FREE LOAN OF BOOKS TO STUDENTS

The tuition and fees used in the cost of attendance for the Pell Grant program does not have to be reduced, if the college loans books to one or more students over the years.

OUTCOME ON SCHEDULED AWARD WITH LOSS OF ELIGIBILITY

When a student loses eligibility to Pell Grant funds prior to disbursement and the student is enrolled at least half-time and has attended one day of classes or more, the college may pay the student at most the amount used for educational purposes before the student lost his/her eligibility. Payment of non-college expenses as rent due for off-campus housing is allowed, if the college decides this to be legitimate cost of attendance.

NON-DISBURSEMENT OF PELL GRANT

When a student does not make acceptable academic progress and the college chooses not to issue a check at the beginning of a payment period but then decides, before the end of the payment period, that the student is progressing satisfactorily, the college may issue a Pell Grant to the student for the whole payment period.

OVERPAYMENT FOR PELL GRANTS

9 The Most Used Awards

Four types of overpayment for Pell Grants are: (1) the student had already received an undergraduate degree; (2) the student was not a citizen; (3) a student drops out of school; (4) an SAI was recalculated and was higher following information used after the payment had been made.

ELIGIBLE AND NON-ELIGIBLE PROGRAMS

A college cannot add the clock hours in an eligible plan to hours in a non-eligible plan and base the Pell Grant on the combined plan.

10 CAMPUS-BASED PROGRAMS

INTRODUCTION

While the deadline for filing the AFSA and MDE forms for federal campus-based programs is the same as the deadline for the Pell Grant Program (May 1). Each participating institution has the option of establishing a priority deadline after which the need of eligible applicants may exceed the funds available. It is possible to consider applications received after the priority deadline, only if funds remain after the needs of eligible students applying before the priority deadline have been met. Find out your school's priority deadline.

Under the regulations governing consumer information, institutions are required to publicize any deadlines or priority dates established.

An eligible student attending two or more institutions simultaneously will be able to receive campus-based aid from both institutions as long as the aid does not exceed the loan limits.

The federal government, through the Department of Education, provides individual schools an amount of money each year to allocate as it chooses to the following three programs.

SUPPLEMENTAL EDUCATIONAL OPPORTUNITY GRANT (SEOG)

An SEOG is also a grant, which does not have to be repaid. To qualify for an SEOG the student must be an undergraduate without a Bachelor's Degree and at least a half time student. However, a school may award SEOGs to a limited number of students who attend school less than half time.

The maximum award is $4000 per year. Selection is based on need and availability of funds. Apply early. This selection is normally made before the Pell Grant.

The award is credited to your account, paid in cash or a combination of the two. The award must be disbursed at least once a school term, unless it is $500 or less. Then it may be paid only once.

STUDY ABROAD

If reasonable study abroad costs exceed the cost of attendance at the home institution, the amount of the grant to be awarded may exceed the $4,000 maximum by as much as $400.

PERKINS LOAN (formerly National Direct Student Loan)

A Perkins Loan is a low-interest loan made by the school's Financial Aid Office for graduate and undergraduate students. The interest rate is 5% and the student has ten years to repay the loan, beginning when the student completes his or her education. Repayment of this loan is made directly to the college or university. The amount of a Perkins Loan may be as much as $2,250 per year, depending on the family's need.

The loan limit for the first two years of school is $4,500. The limit for the last two years is $9,000 minus any money loaned for the first two years. The limit for graduate school is $18,000 minus any money loaned for undergraduate school.

After you sign a promissory note agreeing to repay the loan, the money is credited to your account or paid to you. The loan must be disbursed at least twice a school year.

Selection of recipients is made on the basis of need and availability of funds. Again, you should apply early.

A student enrolled in the summer session is eligible for a Perkins Loan, if they meet the requirements. A student may receive a Perkins Loan for study abroad as long as the program being studied is leading to a degree/certificate at an accredited institution, and the student is eligible for aid.

Repayment begins six months after you leave school. You have up to ten years to repay your school, but the minimum annual repayment is $360 per year. Loan repayments may be deferred for periods during which a borrower: (1) is at least a half-time student; (2) is pursuing a course of study in an approved graduate fellowship program or approved rehabilitation training program for disabled individuals excluding a medical internship or residency program; (3) is unable to find full-time employment, but not in excess of three years; (4) may be suffering an economic hardship, but not in excess of three years; and, (5) is engaged in service described under the cancellation provisions. There are hardship deferments, so check with the repayment office. Heirs should not worry as death cancels repayment as does total disability. Some teaching service cancels repayment; please check.

You must repay this loan. First because it was your promise, second, so that those who come after you will have money to go to school and lastly you otherwise will be letting yourself in for much trouble.

ELIGIBILITY FOR STUDY ABROAD

Students will be eligible for Federal Perkins Loans while engaged in programs of study abroad.

DISCLOSURE REQUIREMENT

An institution is required to provide, at or prior to the time that it makes a loan, written disclosure to a borrower that the disbursement of a loan and the default on a loan will be reported to a credit-bureau organization.

INTERNAL REVENUE SERVICE

In carrying out the provisions of due diligence, the Secretary is authorized to make every effort to ensure that institutions may use the Internal Revenue Service skip-tracing collection procedures on Perkins loans. The Secretary is considering how to implement this new authority.

ANNUAL AND AGGREGATE LOAN LIMITS

The maximum annual loan amount limit for an eligible student attending an institution not participating in the Expanded Lending Option is (1) $5,000 for a graduate or professional student, or (2) $3,000 for a student who has not yet successfully completed a program of undergraduate education.

For an eligible student attending an institution participating in the

Expanded Lending Option, the annual limit is (1) $6,000 for a graduate or professional student, (2) $4,000 for a student who has not yet successfully completed a program of undergraduate education.

The maximum aggregate loan amount for an eligible student attending an institution not participating in the Expanded Lending Option is (1) $30,000 for a graduate or professional student, including loans borrowed as an undergraduate student, or (2) $15,000 for a student who has not yet successfully completed a program of undergraduate study.

For an eligible student attending an institution participating in the Expanded Lending Option, the aggregate limit is (1) $40,000 for a graduate or professional student, including loans borrowed as an undergraduate student, (2) $20,000 for a student who has successfully completed two years of a program leading to a bachelor's degree, but who has not received the degree, or (3) $8,000 for all other students. For a program of study abroad that has reasonable costs in excess of the institution's cost, the annual and aggregate loan limits may be exceeded by 20 percent. The limits for students attending institutions participating in the Expanded Lending Option are not applicable until the award year beginning after July 1, 1993.

STUDENT ELIGIBILITY

A student is required to provide his or her drivers license number, if they have one, at the time of applying for a loan.

UNDERGRADUATE STUDENT ELIGIBILITY

A Student is not ineligible for a loan because he or she has previously received a baccalaureate or professional degree.

ELIMINATION OF DEFENSE OF INFANCY

The "defense of infancy", whereby under applicable law the signing of a contract by a minor would not create a binding obligation, is eliminated. All loans must be made without security or endorsement.

FORBEARANCE

Forbearance may be allowed for all Part E loans (Perkins, Direct, or Defense), whenever made. On receipt of a written request, an institution must grant a borrower forbearance of principal and interest or principal only as requested, renewable at 12-month intervals for a period not to exceed three years (36 months), if the borrower's annual Title IV loan repayment obligation equals or exceeds 20 percent of the borrower's gross income. Forbearance also may be granted if the institution determines that the borrower should qualify for other reasons.

REPAYMENT COMPROMISE

To encourage repayment of defaulted loans, the Secretary may authorize an institution to compromise on the repayment of a loan if the borrower has paid (1) at least 90 percent of the loan, (2) all interest due, and (3) any collection fees due.

CANCELLATION OF LOANS FOR PUBLIC SERVICE

A borrower will continue to receive loan cancellation for service as a full-time teacher in a low-income institution eligible to receive assistance under Chapter 1 of the Education Consolidation and Improvement Act of 1981, as amended. However the Secretary no longer is required to set a 50 percent restriction on low-income institutions in a state receiving assistance under Chapter 1 for cancellation purposes. The Secretary will publish a completely new 1992-93 Low-Income School Directory by the spring of 1993 that will also include the additional qualifying schools and any necessary corrections to the initial 1992-93 Directory. Additionally, if a borrower is teaching in an eligible low-income institution that does not qualify in a subsequent year as a low-income institution, the borrower may continue to teach in that institution and remain eligible to receive a cancellation for service in that institution.

Cancellation provisions are expanded for loans made on or after July 23, 1992 to include the following services as: (1) a full-time special-education teacher, including teachers of infants, toddlers, children, or youth with disabilities in a public or other nonprofit elementary or secondary school system, or as a full-time qualified professional provider of early intervention services in a public or other nonprofit program under public supervision; (2) a full-time teacher of mathematics, science, foreign languages, bilingual education, or any other field of expertise that is determined by the state education agency to have a shortage of qualified teachers; (3) a full-time nurse or medical technician; or, (4) a full-time employee of a public or private nonprofit child or family service agency who is providing or supervising the provision of services to high-risk children and their families from low-income communities.

EXPANDED LENDING OPTION

An Expanded Lending Option (ELO) is created for institutions with default rates of 7.5 percent or less that have executed an ELO participation agreement with the Secretary. Institutions participating in the ELO are required to match the Federal Capital Contribution on a dollar-for-dollar basis and may make loans to students at higher award year and aggregate limits than is the case with non-participating institutions.

INSTITUTIONAL CAPITAL CONTRIBUTION MATCH

An increase in the Institutional Capital Contribution (ICC) to a dollar-for-dollar match with the Federal Capital Contribution (FCC) is established for institutions participating in the Expanded Lending Option program. For any other institution, the ICC will be three-seventeenths of the FCC (or 15 percent of the combined FCC and ICC) in Award Year 1993-94 and one-third of the FCC (or 25 percent of the combined FCC and ICC) for succeeding award years.

EXIT COUNSELING FOR BORROWERS

In addition to the existing exit counseling requirements, each eligible institution must provide counseling to borrowers that includes the terms and conditions under which the student may obtain partial cancellation or defer repayment of principal and interest. If the borrower leaves the institution without the institution's knowledge, the institution must attempt to provide the required information to the borrower in writing. An institution is no longer required to provide information about average indebtedness to students.

Each institution will require that the borrower submit during the exit interview: (1) the borrower's expected permanent address after leaving the institution (regardless of the reason for leaving); (2) the name and address of the borrower's expected employer after leaving the institution; (3) the address of the borrower's records relating to the borrower's name, address, social security number, personal references, and driver's license number.

FEDERAL WORK-STUDY (FWS) PROGRAM

A Student shall not be ineligible for assistance under this division because he or she previously received a baccalaureate or professional degree.

FEDERAL WORK-STUDY (FWS) PROGRAM -- EFFECTIVE OCTOBER 1, 1992

The program name is changed from College Work-Study Program to "Federal Work-Study Program."

PROGRAM PURPOSE

The purpose of the Federal Work-Study (FWS) Program is amended to add an encouragement to students receiving program assistance to participate in community-service activities.

"COMMUNITY SERVICES" DEFINITION

The definition of "community services" is amended to include services in the areas of welfare, social services, transportation, public safety, crime prevention and control, recreation, work in service opportunities or youth corps, specified services for agencies identified in the National and Community Service Act of 1990, support services for student with disabilities, and teaching services.

OVER-AWARD INCOME LIMIT

When a student employed under the FWS Program receives more than $300 in other income from need-based employment that exceeds the student's need, employment under the FWS must be discontinued.

PROGRAM PARTICIPATION AGREEMENT

The agreement between the Secretary and the institution will be amended to add assurances that (1) employment under the program may be used for programs providing supportive services to students with disabilities; and (2) institutions will inform all eligible students of the opportunity to perform community services and will develop and make available information about community-services opportunities.

WORK COLLEGES

Institutions that satisfy the definition of "work-college" may apply to the Secretary to participate in the Work College Program. The term "work-college" means an eligible institution that (1) has been a public or private nonprofit institution with a commitment to community service; (2) has operated a comprehensive work-learning program for at least two years; (3) requires all resident students who reside on campus to participate in a comprehensive work-learning program and the provision of services as an integral part of the institution's educational program and as part of the institution's educational philosophy; and (4) provides students participating in the comprehensive work-learning program with the opportunity to contribute to their education and to the welfare of the community as a whole.

$5,000,000 is authorized to be appropriated for the 1993-94 Award Year to recognize, encourage, and promote the use of comprehensive work-learning programs when they are an integral part of an institution's educational program and are a part of a financial plan that decreases reliance on grants and loans. In additions to the amount authorized to be appropriated, work colleges also may use allocated FWS Program funds and allocated Federal Perkins Loan Program funds to provide flexibility in strengthening the self-help-through-work element in financial aid packaging. Funds made available to work colleges must be matched on a dollar-for-dollar basis from non-Federal sources.

PAYMENTS TO STUDENTS

An institution is authorized to make payments to students for services performed after the academic year but prior to the beginning of the succeeding award year (i.e., for summer employment) from the succeeding award year's allocation. This carry-back authority is in addition to the previous authority to carry-back ten percent of the succeeding year's allocation for use at any time during the preceding award year.

ADMINISTRATIVE EXPENSE ALLOWANCE

The institutional administrative expense allowance for work-study for community-service learning is eliminated; institutions may, however, use up to ten percent of the institution's administrative cost allowance attributable to the FWS Programs expenditures for expenses incurred for its community services program.

The purpose of the College Work-Study Program is to stimulate and promote the part-time employment of students who are enrolled as undergraduate, graduate or professional students who are in need of earnings from employment to pursue courses of study at eligible institutions.

Employment under FWS must be made available to all eligible students in the institution in need, but not exceeding the available funds. Equivalent employment arranged by the institution must be reasonably available, but again not exceeding the available funds.

STUDENT ELIGIBILITY CRITERIA

The institution may award FWS funds to any student who attends less than half-time, if they meet all other eligibility requirements.

A FWS job allows a student to earn part of his or her own school expenses. Usually the student must be going to school at least halftime. However, a school can award FWS jobs to a limited number of students who are enrolled less than halftime. A FWS student may earn as much as $2,000 per year. With this program, a student may earn the minimum wage per hour of work or more, depending on the difficulty of the work. Graduate students may be paid a salary. No student will be paid by commission or fee. Payment is at least once a month. If the FWS award is for $1,000, the job is terminated when that amount has been earned.

The job may be on campus or off campus. If it is on campus, one normally works for the school. If it is off campus, one is likely to work for a government agency or not-for-profit organization. Some schools have agreements with private sector employers however.

On the average, students who work maintain a better grade point record than those that don't. FWS students usually learn to budget their time more effectively.

FWS funds are received from the federal government and administered by the school.

SPECIAL PLANS FOR PUPILS FROM HINDERED SITUATIONS

The law makes available funds "...to identify qualified individuals from disadvantaged backgrounds, to prepare them for a program of post-secondary education, to provide support services for such students who are pursuing programs of post-secondary education, and to train individuals serving or preparing for service in programs and projects so designed." "Student Support Services" (formerly called "Special Services") is one of the services aided by this plan. One of its provisos requires the college to provide each enrolled student in the project "sufficient financial assistance to meet that student's full financial need."

It is not stipulated in the statute which class of aid elements may be used to satisfy the full financial need. A student's full financial need can be met from all sources--parental contribution, student resources, private aid, and State and Federal funds, including potential earnings from Federal Work-Study. FWS regulations allow colleges to install criteria that it sees correct in order to award aid, if the aid is reasonably available to all eligible students who show financial need.

GRADUATE STUDENT ELIGIBILITY

Graduate students are also eligible for the FWS Program. Graduate students must be in compliance with all FWS Program requirements. This includes the requirement that the student be a regular student; that is, enrolled in an eligible program for the purpose of obtaining a degree. Students who are admitted as "special students" or "unclassified graduate students" are not eligible. They must be officially admitted to a <u>degree</u> program in order to be eligible.

The author's daughter participated in the CWS program. She thinks it helped her organize her time and allowed her to meet other students and faculty. When she applied for and got a job after graduation, her employer told her the CWS on her resume' was an asset.

REPAYMENT INFORMATION

The HEA now includes a new provision that defines when the repayment period begins for each of the FFEL programs. The repayment period begins for each of the loan programs as follows: (a) a Federal SLS loan on the day of the last disbursement of the loan proceeds; and (b) a Federal PLUS or Federal Consolidation loan on the day the loan is disbursed. That is, the interest starts to accrue then and is payable in 30 or 90 day increments.

These repayment periods exclude any period in which the borrower is granted an authorized deferment or forbearance.

PROGRAM TO ASSIST BORROWERS IN REPAYING LOANS

The HEA requires the Secretary to undertake a program to encourage private and public-sector employers to assist borrowers in repaying Title IV loans. The Secretary may provide employers with recommended options for payroll deduction of loan payments and loan-repayment employer matching programs as employee benefits.

BORROWER DISCLOSURES

1. **Before Disbursement** - The HEA now provides that prior to or at the time of loan disbursement, the lender must provide the borrower with a clear and concise statement, prominently and clearly displayed in bold print, that the borrower is receiving a loan that must be repaid.

2. **Before Repayment** - The HEA now requires that a lender disclose to the borrower information regarding repayment, as required in S433(b) of the Act, to a Federal Stafford and Federal SLS borrower not less than 60 days

nor more than 240 days before the borrower's first payment is due on the loan.

BANKRUPTCY CLAIMS

The HEA now requires the Secretary to pay the amount of the unpaid balance of principal and interest owed by the borrower on a Federal Stafford (subsidized and unsubsidized), Federal SLS, Federal PLUS, and Federal Consolidation loan when the collection on the loan is stayed in any action under the Bankruptcy Code. The following guidance also applies to FFELP loans on which a stay of collection is in effect on or after July 23, 1992.

If a lender determines that the collection of a borrower's loan has been stayed, the lender should file a bankruptcy claim with the guaranty agency. The guarantee agency must pay the claim within 90 days of the date it is filed. Following payment of the lender's claim, the guaranty agency may submit a bankruptcy claim to the Secretary. However, the agency's payment of a bankruptcy claim to a lender at the Secretary's reimbursement of the agency does not relieve the borrower of the obligation to repay the loan once the bankruptcy action is concluded and the stay of collections is no longer in effect. An FFELP loan generally may not be discharged, unless the borrower has been in repayment status for more than seven years.

DEBT MANAGEMENT OPTIONS FOR HIGH-RISK BORROWERS

The HEA authorizes the Secretary, to the extent funds are appropriated, to provide additional debt-management options for borrowers who are at high risk of default. A high risk of default is determined by performing a FFEL program loan debt to income analysis or assessing other high risk factors identified by the Secretary in regulations.

Under such a program, the Secretary would purchase from the current holders the notes of borrowers who are at high risk of default and who submit a request to the Secretary for an alternative payment option. The alternative repayment options may include graduated or extended repayment options and must include an income-contingent repayment option with the same conditions as the income-contingent program for defaulted borrowers if collections on these loans will increase the net amount the Secretary collects. The Secretary is authorized to enter into contracts or other agreements with private firms or other federal agencies to implement this program. The Department is currently examining how this can be accomplished.

MINIMUM PAYMENT FOR MARRIED COUPLES; MINIMUM PAYMENT OF INTEREST

The reference in prior law to a special minimum loan payment for a married couple has been deleted and a new clause has been inserted that provides that the minimum loan payment by any borrower may not be less than the amount of interest due and payable.

COMMENCEMENT OF REPAYMENT OF FEDERAL SLS LOANS

The statute now requires a lender to offer a borrower of a Federal SLS loan who has also borrowed a Federal Stafford loan the option to defer the beginning of repayment of the Federal SLS loan until six months after the student ceases to be enrolled on at least a half-time basis at an eligible institution. If the borrower chooses this option, interest on the Federal SLS loan will accrue and be paid by the borrower monthly or quarterly or be capitalized no more frequently than quarterly during this period. When notifying the borrower of this option, the lender must also notify the borrower of the option to begin payments earlier than the beginning of the repayment period and provide an explanation of the difference in total cost to the borrower.

COMMENCEMENT OF 10-YEAR REPAYMENT PERIOD

The statute now provides that the 10-year repayment period for a Federal SLS Loan begins at the time the first payment of principal is due from the borrower.

REHABILITATION OF DEFAULTED LOANS

The HEA now requires all guaranty agencies to enter into an agreement with the Secretary to establish a loan rehabilitation program for all borrowers for whom the Secretary has paid a reinsurance claim. For a loan to be eligible to be rehabilitated, the borrower must make 12 consecutive monthly payments. A guaranty agency may not demand that the amount of a borrower's monthly payments exceed an amount that is reasonable and affordable based upon the borrower's total financial circumstances. Until the Secretary can publish regulations containing the criteria a guaranty agency must use in determining a reasonable and affordable payment amount, each agency will be allowed to develop its own criteria. If the borrower's reasonable and affordable monthly payment amount will be less than $50, the agency must document the basis for the determination in the borrower's file.

After the borrower makes 12 consecutive monthly payments, the guaranty agency or Secretary shall, if practicable, sell the loan to an eligible lender. In determining whether a sale is practicable, a guaranty agency should determine whether a borrower who has made 12 consecutive monthly payments is a good candidate for loan rehabilitation. The Secretary does not view an agency's contractual obligations with collection agents, however, as an appropriate factor to consider in determining whether a borrower's loans should be rehabilitated. On sale of the loan to an eligible lender, the borrower is no longer considered to be in default on the loan and regains eligibility for deferments and other program benefits not available to a defaulted borrower. Any lender purchasing a rehabilitated loan must establish a repayment schedule that provides for the borrower to make monthly payments at least as great as the average of the 12 consecutive monthly payments received by the agency.

REINSTATEMENT OF TITLE IV ELIGIBILITY FOR DEFAULTED BORROWERS

The HEA now requires a guaranty agency to establish a program to allow a borrower with one or more defaulted loans to regain eligibility for all Title IV student financial assistance (regardless of whether the defaulted loan has been repurchased by an eligible lender) after the borrower has made six consecutive monthly payments. In determining the monthly payment amount, a guaranty agency may not demand that a borrower make monthly payments that exceed an amount that is reasonable and affordable based upon the borrower's total financial circumstances. Until the Secretary can publish regulations identifying the criteria an agency should use in determining what is reasonable and affordable, the agency may develop and use its own criteria. If the borrower's monthly payment amount will be less than $50, the agency must document the basis for this determination in the borrower's file.

DEMONSTRATION PROJECT FOR BORROWERS IN SELECTED PROFESSIONS OR PERFORMING NATIONAL OR COMMUNITY SERVICE

The Secretary is authorized to establish a demonstration program to assume the obligation to repay a Federal Stafford Loan for any new borrower who enters certain areas of the teaching or nursing professions or performs certain kinds of national or community service. Under the demonstration program, the Secretary will assume portions of the Federal Stafford loan obligations that new borrowers after October 1, 1992 incurred during the last two years of undergraduate education. A borrower is eligible if: (1) he or she is employed as a full-time teacher in certain schools; (2) he or she is employed as a full-time nurse in certain hospitals or health-care centers; or (3) he or she has agreed, in writing, to volunteer for service under the Peace Corps Act or under the Domestic Volunteer Service Act of 1973 or to perform comparable service as a full-time employee of a tax exempt organization under section 501(c)(3) of the Internal Revenue Code of 1986. A borrower performing service as an employee of a tax-exempt organization is eligible if he or she does not receive compensation that exceeds the greater of: (a) The minimum wage rate described in section 6 of the Fair Labor Standards Act of 1938 or (b) an amount equal to 100 percent of the poverty line for a family of two (as defined in section 673(2) of the Community Services Block Grant Act). The Secretary will forgive 15 percent of the borrower's total Stafford loan debt incurred during the borrower's last two years of undergraduate education for the first or second year of service, 20 percent for the third or fourth year of service, and 30 percent for the fifth year of service. The Secretary will promulgate regulations to implement the demonstration program. However, the Department will implement this program only if funding is made available.

DISCHARGE OF FEDERAL PLUS LOANS OF BORROWERS WHEN THE STUDENT DIES

The statute now also provides that a Federal PLUS loan borrower's debt will be discharged by the Secretary if the student, on whose behalf the parent borrowed, dies. This provision applies to any PLUS loan that is in repayment on or after the date of enactment of the amendments.

DURATION OF AUTHORITY TO REPORT FFELP LOAN INFORMATION TO CREDIT BUREAUS

The statute now says a consumer reporting agency may make a report having data received from the Secretary, guaranty agency, or holder of a loan regarding the status of a FFELP loan until:

1. seven years from the date on which the Secretary or guaranty agency paid a claim to the holder of the loan,

2. seven years from the date the Secretary, guaranty agency, eligible lender, or subsequent holder first reported the account as a default to the consumer reporting agency, or

3. for a borrower who enters repayment after defaulting on a loan and defaults again on the loan, seven years from the date the loan enters default the second time.

SIMPLIFICATION OF THE LENDING PROCESS FOR BORROWERS

The HEA has been amended to provide that, to the extent possible, a lender, in cooperation with a borrower, should treat all similar loans made to a borrower under the same section of Title IV, Part B of the HEA as one loan for billing purposes. This includes submitting one bill to the borrower on all loans for a monthly or similar payment period. Also, if a borrower receives a deferment on any of these loans, the deferment is to be extended to the total amount of all of the borrower's loans. Finally, the HEA requires the guaranty agency to make every effort to ensure that the borrower's loans are maintained by one lender, holder, guaranty agency, and servicer to eliminate the need for multiple contacts with the borrower.

STATUTE OF LIMITATIONS ON STUDENT LOAN COLLECTION

The Amendments deleted the sunset provision for the repeal of the statute of limitations of Title IV student loan collections. The repeal had been scheduled to expire on November 15, 1992. As a result, there is no statute of limitations on collection of Title IV student loans.

STAFFORD LOAN PROGRAM

Cut off dates for Federal Stafford Loans (FFELP) applications are established by the individual lending institutions, or the State guarantee agency. It is based on the time required to process the loan to have the check reach the student. This should be prior to the end of the enrollment period covered by the loan.

A Federal Stafford Loan is a low-interest loan made to a family by a lender such as the bank, credit union or savings and loan association. These lending institutions must meet federal standards. The loans are for both undergraduate and graduate students who are going to school at least half-time. The student has ten years after the completion of school to repay the loan. The amount of a Stafford Loan may be as much as $2,625 per year for the first two years, and $4,000 yearly for the last two or three undergraduate years, depending on need. If the student goes to graduate school, he or she can borrow up to $7,500 per year for up to five years. The student does not have to begin repayment on this loan until six months after leaving school. Now please read the next paragraph for new and additional information.

VARIABLE INTEREST RATES FOR NEW FEDERAL STAFFORD LOAN BORROWERS

The HEA now provides that for any Federal Stafford Loan (subsidized or unsubsidized) for which the first disbursement is made on or after October 1, 1992 for a borrower who has no outstanding balance of principal or interest on any FFEL program loan on the date the promissory note is signed, the applicable rate of interest is determined on June 1 of each 12-month period and is equal to the bond equivalent rate of 91-day Treasury bills auctioned at the final auction held prior to June 1, plus 3.1 percent. The applicable interest rate may not exceed 9 percent. Based on this formula, the applicable interest rate for Stafford loans disbursed to such borrowers on or after October 1, 1992 is 6.94 percent. This rate will continue to apply through June 30, 1993. An official notice of this rate will be published in the Federal Register.

REBATES OF EXCESS INTEREST ON FEDERAL STAFFORD LOANS

Excess Interest on Other Federal Stafford Loans to Borrowers with Outstanding Balances

For a Federal Stafford loan (subsidized and unsubsidized) made on or after July 23, 1992 to a borrower who, on the date he or she signs the promissory note has an outstanding balance of principal or interest on any other FFELP (formerly GSLP) loan, the HEA now provides that the borrower is eligible to receive a rebate of excess interest if the sum of the average of the bond equivalent rates of 91-day Treasury bills auctioned for that quarter, plus 3.1 percent, is less than the borrower's applicable interest rate. A borrower who receives a second or subsequent Federal Stafford loan at 8 to 10 percent will be subject to a rebate on the loan both when the borrower's applicable rate is 8 percent and when it increases to 10 percent. A Stafford borrower who has previously borrowed at 7, 8, or 9 percent is eligible for a rebate of excess interest on any new Stafford loan received on or after July 23, 1992. Stafford loans made to new borrowers on or after October 1, 1992 with a variable interest rate are not subject to the requirement to rebate excess interest.

A change in the borrower's status (for example, from in-school status to repayment status where the borrower becomes responsible for interest payments) during a quarter) will require the lender to pro-rate the period to determine correctly the excess interest due to the Secretary and the borrower. The whole matter gets so complex I think the borrower, the lender, and Uncle Sam would all be better off to have let sleeping dogs lie.

ORIGINATION FEE FOR FEDERAL SLS AND FEDERAL PLUS LOANS

The HEA now requires each eligible lender to charge a Federal SLS and Federal PLUS loan borrower an origination fee of 5 percent of the principal amount of the loan. The fee is to be deducted proportionately from each disbursement and paid to the Secretary.

UNSUBSIDIZED FEDERAL STAFFORD LOANS FOR MIDDLE-INCOME BORROWERS

Section 428H has been added to the HEA to provide for unsubsidized Federal Stafford Loans for Middle-Income Borrowers who do not qualify for federal interest subsidies under the Federal Stafford Loan program. Any student who meets the requirements for student eligibility under S484 of the HEA is entitled to borrow an unsubsidized Federal Stafford loan. Guaranty agencies must ensure that all such borrowers are provided with access to unsubsidized Stafford Loans to cover the cost of instruction for periods of enrollment beginning on or after October 1, 1992. For institutions using standard terms, the period of enrollment will be the next scheduled term commencing on or after October 1, 1992 (e.g., semester, quarter, etc.). For institutions not using standard terms, the period of enrollment would include those programs with scheduled start dates on or after October 1, 1992. The terms and conditions of loans made under the subsidized Federal Stafford Loan program apply to unsubsidized Federal Stafford loans made under S428H unless otherwise specified.

The combination of subsidized and unsubsidized Federal Stafford loans for a borrower may not exceed the annual and aggregate limits for loans under the Federal Stafford Loan program. A borrower's unsubsidized Federal Stafford loan amount is determined by calculating the difference between the borrower's cost of attendance for the period of enrollment for which the loan is intended and the amount of estimated financial assistance, including the amount of subsidized Federal Stafford loan for which the borrower qualifies, for the period of enrollment.

An unsubsidized Federal Stafford loan borrower is required to pay a combined origination fee and insurance premium of 6.5 percent on the principal amount of the loan. The cost will be deducted proportionately from each disbursement of the loan.

Borrowers who received unsubsidized Stafford loans under programs that existed prior to the enactment of the Amendments will continue to borrow at the interest rate at which they have borrowed previously.

The provisions of section 428H of the Act are effective for unsubsidized Federal Stafford loans made to cover the cost of instruction for periods of enrollment beginning on or after October 1, 1992.

FEDERAL INSURED STUDENT LOAN (FISL) AND FEDERAL STAFFORD LOAN PROGRAMS - -- VARIOUS EFFECTIVE DATES

A student who is enrolled at an eligible institution or in a program of study abroad that has been approved for credit by an eligible home institution at which the student is enrolled is eligible for the following loan amounts per academic year:

A.(i) A student who has not yet successfully completed the first year of a program of study of undergraduate education as determined by the institution may borrow up to: (a) $2,625 for a program of study that is at least an academic year in length;

(ii) $1,750 for a program of study that is at least two-thirds of an academic year but less than an academic year in length; and

(iii) $875 for a program of study that is at least one-third of an academic year but less than two-thirds of an academic year in length. This change in annual loan limits is effective for loans certified on or after October 1, 1992.

B.(i) A student who has successfully completed the first year of a program of study of undergraduate education but who has not yet successfully completed the rest of the program may borrow up to: (a) $3,500 for a program of study of at least an academic year in length;

(ii) $2,325 for a program of study of at least two-thirds of an academic year but less than an academic year in length; and

(iii) $1,175 for a program of study of at least one-third of an academic year but less than two-thirds of an academic year in length.

This change in annual loan limits is effective for loans for which the first disbursement is made on or after July 1, 1993.

A student who has successfully completed the first and second years of a program of study of undergraduate education but has not successfully completed the remainder of the program may borrow up to:

C.(i) $5,500 for a program of study of at least an academic year in length;

(ii) 3,675 for enrollment in a program of study of at least two-thirds of an academic year but less than an academic year in length; and

(iii) $1,825 for a program of study of at least one-third of an academic year in length but less than two-thirds of an academic year in length.

This change in annual loan limits is effective for loans for which the first disbursement is made on or after July 1, 1993.

For purposes of this provision, an academic year is the institution's academic year, provided it meets the requirement of S481(d). A student who is enrolled in a program of study that normally takes a full-time student two full academic years to complete, based on scheduled time, is not eligible to receive more than an annual loan limit of $3,500 regardless of the time it takes the student to complete the program. If a student is enrolled in a program of study that is longer than one academic year, but less than two academic years in length, the institution must calculate a pro-rated loan amount for the student's second academic year after determining how the remaining balance of the student's program relates to a full academic year. The same approach should be used if the student is in a program greater than two academic years, but less than three academic years in length, greater than three academic years, but less than four academic years in length, and for any other period of enrollment that is less than an academic year in length. The lender may rely upon the information supplied by the institution on loan limit eligibility.

D. A graduate or professional student is eligible to borrow up to $8,500 per academic year.

This provision is effective for loans made to cover the costs of instruction for periods of enrollment beginning on or after October 1, 1993.

A student may borrow up to an aggregate loan maximum amount of $23,000 if the student has not successfully completed a program of undergraduate education, excluding loans obtained under the Federal SLS or Federal PLUS loan programs. A graduate or professional student (as defined in program regulations) may borrow up to an aggregate loan maximum amount of $65,500, including any loans made to the student under the Federal Stafford Loan program before the student became a graduate or professional student, but excluding any loans made under the Federal SLS or Federal PLUS loan programs.

The aggregate loan limit provisions for Federal Stafford loans are effective for loans for which the first disbursement is made on or after July 1, 1993.

REPAYMENT PERIOD

The HEA now includes a new provision that defines when the repayment period begins for each of the FFEL programs. The repayment period begins for each of the loan programs as follows: (a) a Federal Stafford loan on the day after the expiration of the six-month grace period that follows after the student ceases to be enrolled on at least a half-time basis, unless the borrower requests and is granted a repayment schedule that allows the borrower to begin repayment at an earlier date; (b) an unsubsidized Federal Stafford loan, on payments of principal, on the day after the expiration of the six-month grace period that follows after the student ceases to be enrolled on at least a half-time bases, unless the borrower requests and is granted a repayment schedule that allows the borrower to begin repayment at an earlier date. (Payments of interest are the responsibility of the borrower during the in-school and grace periods but may be allowed to accrue and be capitalized.)

These repayment periods exclude any period in which the borrower is granted an authorized deferment or forbearance.

If your need is under $500 you will have a difficult time borrowing money from a bank. They usually do not like to do the paperwork for so small an amount. If you need between $500 and $1,000 you are eligible for a $1,000 loan. If your need is over $1,000 you can borrow the exact amount you need. The bank will subtract a 5% loan origination fee. (Example: on $1,000 loan you receive $950 and the U.S. Government gets $50.) In other words, the bank does not receive the origination fee.

The way the bank makes a profit on these loans is that Uncle Sam pays

10 Campus-based Programs

the interest to the bank until the student begins repayment of the loan.

Lending institutions can set some of their own standards. Sometimes a lending institution will require you to be a depositor. Consequently, you should begin your search for these funds early and not wait until the last moment in case there are criteria you have to meet.

The minimum repayment on a Stafford Loan is $600 per year. The following are two examples of repayment schedules. On a $5,000 loan the 5 year monthly repayment is $103.80, 10 year monthly repayment is $63.34. On a $15,000 loan the 5 year monthly repayment is $311.39. 10 year monthly repayment is $190.02.

Repayment of all federally subsidized loans must be taken seriously. Bankruptcy does not cancel repayment. Death or total disability will cancel the debt. Repayment may be interrupted by service in the Peace Corps or Armed Services.

If you have a hard time meeting your monthly repayment there is another federal agency that can help. This agency consolidates your loans and extends the repayment period by giving you a new loan. The name of the agency is Student Loan Marketing Association (Sallie Mae). You will pay more interest due to the longer length of time, but the payments will be more manageable. Depending on the size of the loan, the repayments may be extended up to 20 years. For more information write Student Loan Marketing Association, Loan Consolidation Program, 1050 Thomas Jefferson St. NW, Ste. 899, Washington, DC 20007. Call 800-872-7834 for more information.

You can apply for a Stafford Loan in the state of your legal residency or in the state where you attend school.

Not all banks, credit unions, and savings and loan institutions participate in the Stafford Loan Program. There is a source to get this information. Contact your state's Department of Higher Education, usually located in the state capital, for the name of the agency that supervises government guaranteed student loans in your state. This agency should be able to tell you the institutions in your area making loans. For your convenience we have listed the current name, address and phone number of these agencies. See Appendix A.

STUDENT ELIGIBILITY REQUIREMENT-STAFFORD LOAN

A student must be enrolled or be accepted to be enrolled at an accredited institution where this will lead a student to a degree/certificate. The student may be an undergraduate, graduate, or professional student. The student must maintain satisfactory progress, must not be in default on a Title IV loan or owe a refund on a Title IV grant.

Before the 1992 amendment to the HEA only students whose need analysis showed a need were able to use this loan. Now, if the stated requirements above are met you can obtain this loan without showing need, but in this case interest debt begins immediately.

STATEMENT OF EDUCATIONAL PURPOSE

Before the loan can be disbursed, the student must file a Statement of Educational Purpose which states that the student will use those funds provided to him/her for expenses that are related to attendance or continued attendance.

STATEMENT OF REGISTRATION STATUS WITH SELECTIVE SERVICE

Before the loan can be disbursed, the student must be registered with selective service or be able to prove that their registration has been waived.

FSLS AND FPLUS IN COORDINATION WITH FEDERAL STAFFORD LOAN (FFELP)

FPLUS Loans, Federal Supplemental Loans for Students(FSLS), state-sponsored or private loans, or non-need-based Income Contingent Loans(ICL) may be used as a substitute for the student's expected family contribution. Before 1993 a student could not use a Federal Stafford Loan (FFELP) as a substitute for the expected family contribution.

FEDERAL PLUS AND FEDERAL SLS INTEREST RATES

The HEA provides that for Federal PLUS and Federal SLS loans for which the first disbursement is made on or after October 1, 1992, the applicable interest rate is determined on July 1 of each 12-month period and is equal to the bond equivalent rate of 52-week Treasury-bills auctioned at the final auction held prior to June 1, plus 3.1 percent. The apropos interest rates on Federal PLUS and SLS loans may not exceed 10 and 11 percent on each. Based on this formula, the applicable variable interest rate for Federal SLS and Federal PLUS loans made on or after October 1, 1992 is 7.36 percent. This rate will continue to apply through June 30, 1993. An official notice of this rate will be published in the Federal Register.

LIMITATIONS ON INTEREST PAID TO LENDERS PRIOR TO DISBURSEMENT OF A LOAN

The HEA provides that a lender may not receive interest on a loan that is disbursed by check for any period earlier than 10 days prior to the first disbursement of the loan, or earlier than 3 days prior to the first disbursement to the loan for loans disbursed by electronic funds transfer (EFT). The Secretary interprets the use of the term "disbursement" in this context to mean delivery of the loan to the borrower by the institution.

If the borrower's application shows no prior loan and the borrower is reported as being in grade level 1, the lender may assume that the borrower's loan is subject to delayed delivery.

The first disbursements for new borrowers subject to delayed delivery for loans disbursed by check is to be the 21st day of the borrower's period of enrollment. Disbursement of funds by EFT is to be the 28th day of the borrower's period of enrollment.

CONTINUING BORROWERS

Loans disbursed to continuing borrowers by check should be issued 10 days prior to the first day of the
borrower's period of enrollment. If the funds are disbursed by EFT, then the 24th day prior to the borrower's period of enrollment is the issuance day.

NOTIFICATION OF BORROWER REPAYMENT PERIOD

The HEA now provides that a guaranty agency must require its lenders to notify borrowers, no later than 120 days after the borrower has left the eligible institution, of the date on which the repayment period on their loans begins.

NOTIFICATION OF LOAN SALES AND TRANSFERS

The HEA now requires that if a loan is sold, transferred, or assigned to another holder and there is a change in the identity of the party to whom the borrower must send ensuing payments or direct any communications concerning the loan, then both the transferor and transferee must, within 45 days from the date the transferee acquires a legally enforceable right to receive payment from the borrower on the loan, separately notify the borrower of: 1) the sale or other transfer; 2) the identity of the transferee; 3) the name and address of the party to who subsequent payments or communications must be sent; and 4) the telephone numbers of both the transferor and transferee. The notifications from the transferor and transferee may not be mailed in the same envelope. The telephone number of a loan servicer acting as an agent in lieu of the lender must be available to the borrower. This provision is identical to the requirements of the earlier law, except that the law now requires that a separate notice must be sent to the borrower by each party to the sale or transfer. The Department will amend the regulations to reflect the statutory requirement.

The HEA also now requires that if a loan is sold, transferred, or assigned to another holder, the transferor must notify the guaranty agency of the sale, transfer, or assignment and must provide the agency with the address and telephone number by which contact may be made with the holder. Such notifications should take place within 45 days of the date the transferee acquires a legally enforceable right to receive a payment from the borrower.

Finally, upon the request of an institution, the guaranty agency must notify the last institution the student attended (prior to the beginning of the repayment period on the loan) of any sale, transfer, or assignment of the loan to another holder and the address and telephone number by which contact may be made with the new loan holder concerning repayment of the loan. This rule only applies if the borrower is in a grace period or in repayment status.

FORBEARANCE - Mandatory Provisions for Medical Interns/residents

The statutory provision governing forbearance for borrowers serving in medical internships/residencies has been amended to provide that a forbearance for these borrowers must be the temporary cessation of all payments unless the borrower requests forbearance in the form of an extension of time for making payments or making smaller payments than were previously scheduled.

FORBEARANCE - for Borrowers Generally

The provision governing forbearance for borrowers generally has been amended to prescribe that the forbearance must be a temporary cessation of all payments unless the borrower requests forbearance in the form of an extension of time for making payments or making smaller payments than were previously scheduled.

SALES AND TRANSFERS OF LOANS PRIOR TO DISBURSEMENT PROHIBITED

The HEA has been amended to prohibit a lender from selling or transferring a promissory note for any FFEL program loan until the final disbursement of the loan has been made. However, the sale or transfer may take place if the transaction does not result in a change in the identity of the party to who payments on the loan will be made and the first disbursement of the loan has been made.

GRADUATED OR INCOME-SENSITIVE REPAYMENT

The HEA now requires that not more than six months prior to the due date of the first payment on a Federal Stafford or Federal SLS Loan, a lender must offer a FFEL program borrower the option of repaying the loan according to a graduated or income-sensitive repayment schedule established by the lender in accordance with regulations promulgated by the Secretary. To comply with this requirement, the lender must provide both options to the borrower.

This requirement applies to loans for which the first disbursement is made on or after July 1, 1993 to new borrowers on the date the borrower applies for a loan.

ANNUAL AND AGGREGATE LOAN LIMITS - FEDERAL SUPPLEMENTAL LOANS FOR STUDENTS

The HEA establishes the following annual limits a student may borrow under the Federal SLS program in any academic year or for a period of seven consecutive months, whichever is longer:

1. For a student who has not yet successfully completed the first and second year of a program of undergraduate education:

(a) $4,000 for a program of study that is at least an academic year in length;

(b) $2,500 for a program of study that is at least two-thirds of a academic year but less than an academic year in length;

(c) $1,500 for a program of study that is less than two-thirds but at least one-third of an academic year in length.

2. For a student who has successfully completed the first and second years of a program of study of undergraduate education, but who has not yet completed the remainder of the program, up to:

(a) $5,000 for a program of study that is at least an academic year in length;

(b) $3,325 for a program of study that is at least two-thirds of an academic year but less than an academic year in length; and

(c) $1,675 for a program of study that is at least one-third of an academic year but less than two-thirds of an academic year in length.

A graduate or professional student, as defined in the Department's regulations, may borrow up to $10,000 per academic year.

For purposes of this provision, an academic year is the institution's stated academic year. A student enrolled in a program of study that normally takes a full-time student two full academic years to complete, based on scheduled time, is restricted to a $4,000 annual loan limit regardless of the time it takes the student to complete the program. If a student is enrolled in a program of study that is longer than one academic year, but less than two academic years in length, the institution must calculate a pro-rated loan amount for the students's second academic year according to the schedule of loan limits provided above after determining how the remaining balance of the student's program relates to a full academic year. This same approach should be used if the student is in a program greater than two academic years, but less than three academic years in length, greater than three academic years, but less than four academic years in length, and for any other period of enrollment that is less than an academic year in length. The lender may rely upon the information supplied by the institution on the loan limit eligibility.

The aggregate insured principal amount of Federal SLS loans an undergraduate student may borrow, excluding any capitalized interest, may not exceed $23,000. A graduate or professional student may borrow up to an aggregate maximum insured principal amount of $73,000, excluding the amount of capitalized interest. The aggregate maximum amount for a graduate or professional student includes any amount received for study at the undergraduate level.

This change applies to loans for which the first disbursement is made on or after July 1,1993.

FEDERAL PLUS LOAN DEFERMENT BASED ON DEPENDENT'S STATUS

The Amendments eliminate the deferment previously available to PLUS borrowers on the basis of the status of the borrower's dependent. This change applies to new borrowers whose first disbursement on a loan takes place on or after July 1, 1993. "Old" borrowers would continue to receive deferments under this provision.

PROVISIONS EFFECTIVE JULY 1, 1993, FEDERAL PLUS PROGRAMS, REVISED ELIGIBILITY

The eligibility requirements for the Federal PLUS Program in the HEA have been revised. A parent no longer will be eligible to borrow on behalf of a dependent student if the parent is determined, based on criteria established by federal regulations, to have an adverse credit history. This provision applies to loans for which the first disbursement is made on or after July 1, 1993.

REPEAL OF LOAN LIMITS

The annual and aggregate limits in the HEA on the amount a parent may borrow on behalf of a dependent student have been repealed. This change applies to all Federal PLUS loans for which the first disbursement is made on or after July 1, 1993. However, a Federal PLUS loan may not exceed the student's estimated cost of attendance minus any estimated financial assistance the student has been or will be awarded during the period of enrollment.

FEDERAL PLUS LOAN DISBURSEMENT

The Act requires that all Federal PLUS loans for which the first disbursement is made on or after October 1, 1992 must be disbursed by either electronic transfer of funds (EFT) from the lender to the eligible institution or by a check that is co-payable to the institution and the parent borrower.

Co-payable Federal PLUS checks must be disbursed to the institution. The institution must verify the student's eligibility prior to forwarding the Federal PLUS check to the borrower. The institution is not required to provide its endorsement on the check before forwarding it to the borrower. Lenders must provide the institution the name and social security number of the student on whose behalf the parent is borrowing on the check or on an attached roster. As with student borrowers, in the case of loan proceeds disbursed by EFT, the institution is required to collect an authorization form the parent to release funds from the institution's EFT escrow account for delivery to the borrower. The institution must retain a copy of the authorization in the file of the student on whose behalf the parent is borrowing.

If you are not eligible for the Federal Stafford Loan, you are probably eligible for the FPLUS or FSLS. These loans are not as attractive because there is only a 60 day grace period before you must start paying the monthly interest.

Normally, the PLUS loans are available when you cannot qualify for other sources, or when other sources have been exhausted. If the student is a dependent student the parents may use the PLUS Loan to borrow up to $4,000 a year. The total loan amount per child is $20,000. The student must be enrolled at least half time. A Need Analysis does not have to be administered as with the Stafford Loan in order to qualify for the PLUS. However, the borrower does have to prove to be credit-worthy.

Suppose the PLUS borrower does *not* prove credit-worthy. Then the law says the dependent student now qualifies for the SLS (Supplemental Loans for Students).

Independent undergraduate and graduate students may borrow up to $4,000 a year under the SLS. There is a limit of $20,000 in this program, but this is in addition to the Stafford Loan. But remember, you can borrow no more than what the school figures is your "cost of education". For example, if the school figures your cost of education is $8,000 and you receive a Pell Grant for $1,000, an SEOG for $1,500, and a Stafford Loan for $2,625, then you are limited to $2,875 in the PLUS or SLS.

The borrower of the SLS must take the "needs analysis" to first discover if they are eligible for Pell or Stafford. The interest rate on either loan is set in June for the following school year, and is indicated on your promissory note. Presently, it is running around 10%.

Some states float bonds to furnish students loan moneys for Stafford, PLUS and SLS at lower than commercial rates. Check with your state educational agency for this information. They are listed in Appendix A in this book.

INCOME-CONTINGENT REPAYMENT FOR DEFAULTED BORROWERS

The HEA provides that the Secretary may promulgate regulations establishing income-contingent repayment of FFEL programs loans, except for Federal PLUS loan. Income-contingent repayment would be required for loans for which: (1) the promissory notes contain a notice that it is subject to income-contingent repayment; and (2) the loans have been assigned to the Secretary following default.

The Secretary may publish regulations to establish the terms and conditions of the income-contingent repayment program. Those regulations must specify the schedules under which the borrower's income will be assessed for repayment of loans, must permit the discharge of the debt not later than 25 years after commencement of income-contingent repayment, and may provide for the potential collection of amounts in excess of the principal and interest on the original loan.

To implement income-contingent repayment, the Secretary must issue a formal finding that a collection mechanism is available that assures a high degree of certainty of collection of these loans and that income-contingent repayment strategies will increase the net amount the Secretary will collect. The Department is currently examining how this can be accomplished.

11 LOAN CONSOLIDATION

FEDERAL CONSOLIDATION LOAN PROGRAM - Effective January 1, 1993

BORROWER ELIGIBILITY

The Amendments have made some changes to Federal Consolidation loan eligibility to provide that a borrower, at the time of application, must:

(a) have a minimum debt under the eligible loan programs of at least $7,500; and

(b) be in a grace period or repayment status on all loans being consolidated; or

(c) if in a delinquent or default status, will reenter repayment through loan consolidation.

A borrower may consolidate loans made under the FISL, Federal Stafford, Perkins, Federal PLUS, Federal SLS, and Health Professions Student Loan (HPSL) programs. A loan on which a borrower defaulted is eligible for consolidation only if the borrower has, prior to the time of application, made satisfactory repayment arrangements with the holder of the loan and provides evidence of the arrangements to the consolidating lender.

The HEA now allows a Federal Consolidation loan borrower to add any eligible loans received before the date of consolidation to an existing Consolidation Loan, provided they are added within 180 days of the date the Federal Consolidation loan is made.

These changes apply to Federal Consolidation loans for which the application is received by the lender on or after January 1, 1993.

CONSOLIDATION OF LOANS OF MARRIED COUPLES

The HEA now allows a married couple to consolidate their individual loans if they agree to be held jointly and severally liable for repayment without regard to the amount of their individual indebtedness and any future change in their marital status.

11 Loan Consolidation

For a married couple to be eligible for consolidation, only one spouse needs to meet the eligibility requirements for a Consolidation Loan. However, each spouse must certify that he or she does not have another application for a Federal Consolidation Loan pending and each must agree to notify the holder of the loan of any change of address.

DEFERMENT PROVISIONS FOR FEDERAL CONSOLIDATION LOAN BORROWERS

The HEA has been amended to provide that, during authorized deferment periods, interest will accrue on a Federal Consolidation Loan and be paid by the Secretary.

REPAYMENT SCHEDULE FOR FEDERAL CONSOLIDATION LOANS

The HEA now requires lenders to offer repayment schedules on Consolidation Loans that provide for graduated or income-sensitive repayment. The length of the repayment period, as determined by the total amount of the borrower's Federal Consolidation Loans and other student loan debts, has also been amended. If the sum of the borrower's Federal Consolidation Loans and the amount outstanding on other student loans owed by a borrower is: (1) $7,500 or more but less than $10,000, the term is not more than 12 years, (2) $10,000 or more but less than $20,000, the term is not more than 15 years, (3) $20,000 or more but less than $40,000, the term is not more than 20 years, (4) 40,000 or more but less than $60,000, the term is not more than 25 years, 5) 60,000 or more, the term is 30 years.

DEFERMENT PROVISIONS FOR FEDERAL FAMILY EDUCATION LOANS

As previously noted, effective on enactment of the Amendments, for purposes of an in-school deferment, an eligible institution is defined as including any institution, whether it is participating in any Title IV program or has lost its eligibility to participate in the FFEL program because of a high default rate. If an institution has never participated in the Title IV programs previously, the institution must request a determination from the Secretary that it satisfies the definition of an eligible institution prior to certifying borrower deferment forms.

11 Loan Consolidation

The following deferments will be applicable to any borrower under the Federal Stafford, Federal SLS, and Federal PLUS loan programs who is a new borrower on the date he or she applies for a loan and whose first disbursement of such loan is made on or after July 1, 1993:

1. Periods during which the borrower is pursuing at least a half-time course of study as determined by an eligible institution.

2. Periods during which the borrower is pursuing a course of study under a graduate fellowship program or a rehabilitation training program for disabled individuals approved by the Secretary.

3. Up to three years during periods in which the borrower is seeking and unable to find full-time employment.

4. Up to three years for any reason, which the lender determines, under regulations prescribed by the Secretary, has caused or will cause the borrower to have an economic hardship.

An economic hardship exists when the borrower is working full-time and is earning an amount that does not exceed the greater of the minimum wage or the poverty line for a family of two as determined in accordance with the Community Service Block Grant Act or if the borrower meets other criteria established by the Secretary in regulations.

These deferment provisions also apply to any borrower with a Federal Consolidation loan made on or after July 1, 1993 if the borrower has no other outstanding FFELP loans. Prior to the effective date for these provisions, all borrowers, including new ones receiving unsubsidized Federal Stafford Loans on or after October 1, 1992 will qualify for the existing deferment provisions. These provisions will continue to apply to old borrowers after July 1, 1993 for the life of borrower's loan.

DEFERMENT ELIGIBILITY FOR BORROWERS ENGAGED IN GRADUATE FELLOWSHIP PROGRAMS OUTSIDE THE UNITED STATES

The deferment provisions for new borrowers continue to contain a deferment for borrowers engaged in graduate fellowship programs outside the United States.

The HEA provides that on the date of application an individual who is a new borrower may defer repayment of FFELP loans for the complete period of graduate or post-graduate fellowship-supported study (such as pursuant to a Fullbright grant) outside the United States. This provision applies to loans made on or after July 1, 1993.

TEACHER SHORTAGE AREA DEFERMENT

The Amendments have deleted the deferment provided previously to full-time teachers in targeted teacher shortage areas. This change applies to new borrowers who first disbursement on a loan is made on or after July 1, 1993 and deletes the requirements in the FFELP program for establishing teacher shortage areas. "Old" borrowers will remain eligible for this deferment for the life of their loans based on targeted shortage areas identified under criteria established in the Paul Douglas Teacher Scholarship Program."

12 HOW TO INCREASE GOVERNMENTAL FINANCIAL AID

SAMPLE SITUATION #1

Mr. A is salaried at $18,000 a year, but he has $50,000 in a CD from an accident settlement. His child cannot, at present, qualify for governmental college grants. His certificate of deposit is an asset. He has more than $30,000 in assets. His CD makes him $1,500 a year. His taxable income is $19,500.

He could put all or part of his CD in a Single Premium Deferred Annuity. He could lower his assets enough this way to qualify for a Pell Grant and he would lower his income tax bill. He might also qualify for an SEOG.

SAMPLE SITUATION #2

The student's parents are divorced. The family unit who provides support is the unit considered in qualifying for financial aid. For example, if the student lives with mother and step-father, the step-father's and mother's income will be considered in qualifying for state and federal funds.

Mrs. B has a taxable income of $25,000 a year. She is the sole support of her child. Her only asset is her house. It would be grabbed up at $70,000. Her remaining mortgage is $35,000. Her total assets are thus $35,000, but now a home is not considered an asset for Federal College Aid. (See page 18.) It is possible to take out a second mortgage, say for $14,000, and put $3,000 in a Single Premium Deferred Annuity. She will build up a retirement with this policy. Her note on her car is $7,000. She can pay off this note, and put the monthly car payment to reduce her second mortgage. She has $4,000 in other consumer debt that is also paid off. Now her assets, for those awarders that consider the home, will be below the cut-off amount. Her salary needs to come down, so if the firm she is working for offers a cafeteria plan for health insurance, etc., she should use this to subtract such items from her income. Now the student is eligible for more funds than before.

WHAT TO DO WITH ASSETS

There are instruments into which Mr. A and Mrs. B, or anyone else for that matter, can place their assets so they will not be considered assets. If these assets were originally income producing assets these instruments will also help lower the income and the income tax paid. But you should start these actions well before your child is set to go off to college.

UNIVERSAL LIFE

The instrument to which I refer is a Universal Life Insurance Policy. In effect, this instrument has two parts to it. One is term insurance in units of $10,000, and the other part is tax deferred savings, paying 7-7.25% compounded annually. If your child is going to school, this is a time you need more life insurance protection and need to lower your assets.

If, heaven forbid, the death benefits are paid, the whole amount is not subject to income tax as long as the beneficiary is not your estate, but an individual(s). Your agent can set your premiums so that in eight years your interest will more than cover your premium. You then can choose to stop paying premiums or to borrow against the policy. Choose a strong insurance company.

YOUR BUSINESS IS AN IDEAL ASSET SHELTER

If you already own your own business, you are probably already familiar with how to use it for a tax and asset shelter. If you are not, please read on.

If you have wanted to start your own business, now might be the time to do so. Most small businesses show a small profit or loss their first few years. Not necessarily an actual loss, but a paper loss.

For instance, suppose you office in your home. Your office space is worth $200 a month. Your share of utilities is $75 per month, telephone (listed in the business name) $50, supplies $40, auto $50, upkeep $50, etc. Suppose the deductible expenses totals $400 per month. That's a $4,800 a year deduction. The house and utility expense are not deductible if the business shows a loss. Suppose your income from the business is $800 per month or $9,600 that year.

Furthermore, suppose you hire your college bound child to work for you. You can deduct his/her salary expense. You must pay a wage that is in line with the work that they do. That is to say that you cannot pay an exorbitantly high wage. The IRS would consider that a tax dodge. Suppose over forty-eight weeks you pay him/her $4,800. Now, over the years, he/she can save money for college, buy their own clothes and maybe a used car to go off to school.

If you have a hobby you have been involved in for years, you may be able to turn that into a very profitable business.

If you have unique products to sell, you can start a mail order business from your home. There are hundreds of books on ideas for businesses and how to make them grow. With the tax structure the way it is, it is advantageous to own your own business, no matter how small. (See page 14, "HOW ARE ASSETS EVALUATED")

13 STATE GRANTS

STATE STUDENT INCENTIVE GRANT (SSIG) PROGRAM -- EFFECTIVE FOR THE 1993-94 AWARD YEAR

The statute authorizes $105,000,000 for fiscal year 1993 and such sums as may be necessary for the next four succeeding fiscal years.

The maximum award under the SSIG Program increases from $2,500 to $5,000.

To be eligible for SSIG funds, a state program must ensure that no student or parent will be charged a fee payable to an entity other than the state for the collection of data to make a determination of that student's financial need.

The statute provides that, if a state's allocation under the SSIG Program is based in part on the financial need of independent students or less than full-time students, a reasonable proportion of the state's allocation must be made available to those students.

A student who is participating in a program of study abroad that is approved for credit by the institution of higher education at which he or she is enrolled is an eligible student for the SSIG Program.

For more detailed information on state grants see "DON'T MISS OUT" by Robert & Anna Leider, Chapter 11.

THE TYPES OF STATE GRANTS

1. Grants awarded on basis of need for study in your state of residence.

2. Same as above except usually in a contiguous state with whom your state has signed reciprocity agreements.

3. Awards (Merit) based on academic accomplishments. For some you must show financial need; others are merit alone. States are increasing the merit awards faster than the need awards. Each state would like to

13 State Grants

keep the better students in the state. Remember that if you are trying to improve the types of your awards.

4. Special loans for students, different from the federal loans, are used in some states. Usually the money is generated by selling tax exempt bonds in that state. In or out of state students enrolling in these participating colleges in this state are eligible for these loans.

5. Awards are given for students who will teach subjects in which there is a shortage, such as math and science, or who will teach in geographical areas short of teachers like the inner cities or rural areas. Awards must be repaid if your commitment to teach is not fulfilled.

6. Special fields in which the states believe it has a shortage. It may be medicine, nursing, bilingual education, special education, etc. Graduate programs are included in this class.

7. Minority Group Program, Blacks, Latinos and Native Americans.

8. Work Study, a state program similar to the federal program.

9. Veterans who are residents of the state and served during a time of hostility.

10. National Guard benefits for serving in the state's National Guard in addition to the federal benefits.

11. Dependent of disabled or deceased veteran.

12. Dependent of POW or MIA.

13. Dependent of fireman or police killed on duty.

14. Dependents of Military can in some states attend college in that state at a reduced tuition rate.

15. Some states let families purchase "Baccalaureate Bonds" to help families to prepare for college costs. The income from these bonds is tax

13 State Grants

exempt if that money is used to pay college costs. When available these bonds can be purchased through banks and brokerage houses. There is also the "prepaid tuition plan" which allows families to freeze the cost of tuition by either making a lump sum investment or making regular payments. Usually the state invests this money and then pays the student's tuition whenever he or she enters college. This means the state takes the risk of guaranteeing the students tuition.

The student should look in the appendix for the state agency phone number. Contact this agency for a listing of **state** grants. Realize that you must call the Veterans Administration to find out about veterans awards, the state national guard etc. depending on the type of award. Also do realize that these awards do change with time.

NAME OF AGENCY   PHONE

STATE TYPE OF AWARD

Some questions you might want to ask are:

1. Does your state have a reciprocal agreement with contiguous states so that a resident of one state can pay in-state tuition rates while attending school in that adjoining state?

2. Does your state provide need based assistance to residents going to an out of state school?

3. How and when do you apply for state awards?

4. How do I contact the state rehabilitation agency for college aid when I am physically impaired?

TEXAS STATE GRANTS

STATE TUITION AID PROGRAM Most states have a tuition aid program, which may award as much as $2,200 per year. This does not have to be repaid. The tuition Aid Program (TAP) award is based on the family's net taxable income during the previous year, and on the tuition charge at the institution the student attends. Generally, a family with a net taxable income of more than $25,000 would not qualify for a TAP.

PUBLIC EDUCATIONAL GRANT(PEG) To be eligible for this campus-based program, the student must show financial need and be enrolled in a public institution participating in the PEG program. Applications may be obtained through the director of financial aid at any participating public institution.

STATE SCHOLARSHIP PROGRAM FOR ETHNIC RECRUITMENT (SSER) Each participating institution matches its state allocation and uses the money for scholarships and for recruiting resident minority students enrolling for the first time either as freshmen or new transfer students. A student whose ethnic group comprises less than 40% of the enrollment at a particular school may be eligible for a scholarship from that school. To qualify, entering freshmen must score at least 800 on the SAT or at least 18 on the ACT, and transfer students must have a GPA of at least 2.75. A judgement of financial need by the financial aid director at the institution and recommendations of the admissions officer or minority students affairs officer help determine eligibility for the scholarship. Interested minority students should contact the financial aid director at the public senior college in which they plan to enroll.

13 State Grants

THINGS TO CONSIDER

The family should contact the chosen school's Financial Aid Administrator to determine which programs that school participates in. The family should also investigate any private or commercial sources of aid that might be available.

14 NON-GOVERNMENTAL LOANING SOURCES

Four of the more popular educational loan programs are described below.

An investment in education pays dividends for life.

Here are two easy, sure ways to finance that investment.

For many years Chemical Banking Corporation-one of America's largest bank holding companies-has been committed to providing convenient, long-term financing to help families cope with the high cost of education.

Today, a year at top school can cost $10,000, $15,000, or more. Even with scholarships, government loans, and other financial aid, many families cannot meet these costs without additional help.

Chemical's Educational Financing Group offers government-backed unsecured loans, alternative loan programs, and a budget program to help meet this need.

Two of these options available from Chemical are our unsecured and non-governmental loan programs designed to assist parents and students in meeting the ever-rising costs of education:

* The Educational Line of Credit-a check activated line of credit based on a variable interest rate.

* The Educational Loan Program of the Tuition Plan-A fixed rate loan program based on convenient repayment terms, with the funds disbursed semester by semester.

Over the years, hundreds of thousands of students have been able to attend the educational institution of their choice through the convenient financing they received from the Educational Financing Group. The information in this brochure can help you to select the program that best fits your needs.

The Educational Financing Group-The commitment continues.

The Educational Line of Credit (ELC) A Check-Activated Variable Interest Rate Loan Program

The concept-The Educational Line of Credit (ELC) provides the borrower with a revolving line of credit. Using a book of personalized checks, the borrower pays school expenses by drawing against the line of credit.

The ELC is available at a competitive, variable interest rate. The annual Percentage Rate (A.P.R.) is only 4.50% above the last highest Prime Rate as published in The Wall Street Journal and can change on a quarterly basis. This rate is competitive with other unsecured loans. For example, if the Prime Rate on November 15th is 6.50%, the APR on January 1st would be 11.00%.

The ELC may be used for tuition, room and board, transportation and any other education-related expenses-on any level from elementary through graduate or professional study.
The ELC may be used by parents, grandparents, guardians or others willing to finance the education of a student.

The school is not involved in the ELC because your agreement is a private contract between you and Chemical. The personalized checks are sent directly to the borrower, providing a confidential financial service.

Finance charges are low because checks are written and charges incurred only when the fund are needed and used. Most personal loans distribute funds once and charge interest on the full amount of the loan.

The annual expense for an ELC is low because the ONLY costs for an ELC are principal and interest. There are no origination fees, application fees, closing costs, administrative or other charges. Some alternative financing programs charge an origination fee, while other types of loans, such as Home Equity Loans, require legal fees, a title search, points, mortgage tax and other closing costs which drive up the total amount of money borrowed.

Life insurance covering the entire unpaid balance is provided at no additional cost because Chemical wants to give the student and the borrower the peace of mind they deserve.

14 Non-governmental Loaning Sources

The limits to the ELC are a $5,000 minimum credit line ($2,500 for prep schools) and you may borrow $10,000, $20,000 or more. The minimum check is $250.00. For any given academic year, funds which can be drawn upon may not exceed the total amount of the ELC divided by the number of years of study it covers.

The minimum amount repaid each month is determined by dividing the outstanding balance as of the last advance by 84, plus finance charges. (This term may be shorter on loans used for preparatory schools.) The minimum payment may be exceeded at any time. Repayment begins 45 days after the funds are drawn from ELC.

The Educational Loan Program of the Tuition Plan*-A Fixed-Rate Loan on Convenient Terms

The Concept-The Educational Loan Program of the Tuition Plan, a company of Chemical Banking Corporation is a fixed rate loan program designed to provide as much money as needed each academic year to pay for a student's course of study, depending on any local restrictions.

The loan may be used for any student for any education-related expense.

The loan may be used by any student enrolled in any preparatory school, college or graduate school in the United States.

The money may be borrowed by anyone willing to finance the education of that student.

The amount of money borrowed is based on the ability of the borrower to repay.

Low cost credit life insurance is available in most states and offered on an optional basis. The insurance will pay the amount of money not repaid, plus it covers all scheduled funds not yet disbursed.

The amount of money repaid each month is determined by the length of the educational program being financed. For the current interest rate for the Tuition Plan Loan Program, call 1-800-258-3640.

Finance charges are reduced because charges are only incurred when

14 Non-governmental Loaning Sources

the funds are needed and used.

There are no origination or application fees or any other charges.

The school is not involved in the Tuition Plan Loan.

It's easy to apply for a Tuition Plan Loan or a Chemical ELC. Simply complete and mail the postage-paid application attached. Please indicate which unsecured loan option you would like to be considered for. If you desire Credit Life Insurance on the Tuition Plan Loan, please indicate so on the application. Further information will follow.

For quick processing please include some form of income verification. This includes a W-2 Form or Pay Statement and for self-employed applicants, the last two years' signed tax returns. If you have any questions regarding this or any other Educational Financing Group Plan, call toll-free (1-800-258-3640).

Chemical's Educational Financing Group offers the following programs:
Chemical Bank

* Federal Stafford Loans (subsidized and unsubsidized)
* Federal Supplemental Loans for Students
* Federal Plus Loans
* Alumni Advantage (Federal Loan Consolidation)
* Educational Line of Credit The Tuition Plan
* Educational Loan Program
* Educational Financing Manager

For information on any of these programs, please call toll-free 1-800-258-3640.

* An investment in education pays dividends for life.

Here are two easy, sure ways to finance that investment.

For many years Chemical Banking Corporation-one of America's largest bank holding companies-has been committed to providing convenient, long-term financing to help families cope with the high cost of education.

14 Non-governmental Loaning Sources

Today, a year at top school can cost $10,000, $15,000, or more. Even with scholarships, government loans, and other financial aid, many families cannot meet these costs without additional help.

Chemical's Educational Financing Group offers government-backed unsecured loans, alternative loan programs, and a budget program to help meet this need.

Two of these options available from Chemical are our unsecured and non-governmental loan programs designed to assist parents and students in meeting the ever-rising costs of education:

* The Educational Line of Credit-a check activated line of credit based on a variable interest rate.

* The Educational Loan Program of the Tuition Plan-A fixed rate loan program based on convenient repayment terms, with the funds disbursed semester by semester.

Over the years, hundreds of thousands of students have been able to attend the educational institution of their choice through the convenient financing they received from the Educational Financing Group. The information in this brochure can help you to select the program that best fits your needs.

The Educational Financing Group-The commitment continues.

The Educational Line of Credit (ELC) A Check-Activated Variable Interest Rate Loan Program

The concept-The Educational Line of Credit (ELC) provides the borrower with a revolving line of credit. Using a book of personalized checks, the borrower pays school expenses by drawing against the line of credit.

The ELC is available at a competitive, variable interest rate. The annual Percentage Rate (A.P.R.) is only 4.50% above the last highest Prime Rate as published in The Wall Street Journal and can change on a quarterly basis. This rate is competitive with other unsecured loans. For example, if the Prime Rate on November 15th is 6.50%, the APR on January 1st

14 Non-governmental Loaning Sources

would be 11.00%.

The ELC may be used for tuition, room and board, transportation and any other education-related expenses-on any level from elementary through graduate or professional study.
The ELC may be used by parents, grandparents, guardians or others willing to finance the education of a student.

The school is not involved in the ELC because your agreement is a private contract between you and Chemical. The personalized checks are sent directly to the borrower, providing a confidential financial service.

Finance charges are low because checks are written and charges incurred only when the fund are needed and used. Most personal loans distribute funds once and charge interest on the full amount of the loan.

The annual expense for an ELC is low because the ONLY costs for an ELC are principal and interest. There are no origination fees, application fees, closing costs, administrative or other charges. Some alternative financing programs charge an origination fee, while other types of loans, such as Home Equity Loans, require legal fees, a title search, points, mortgage tax and other closing costs which drive up the total amount of money borrowed.

Life insurance covering the entire unpaid balance is provided at no additional cost because Chemical wants to give the student and the borrower the peace of mind they deserve.

The limits to the ELC are a $5,000 minimum credit line ($2,500 for prep schools) and you may borrow $10,000, $20,000 or more. The minimum check is $250.00. For any given academic year, funds which can be drawn upon may not exceed the total amount of the ELC divided by the number of years of study it covers.

The minimum amount repaid each month is determined by dividing the outstanding balance as of the last advance by 84, plus finance charges. (This term may be shorter on loans used for preparatory schools.) The minimum payment may be exceeded at any time. Repayment begins 45 days after the funds are drawn from ELC.

14 Non-governmental Loaning Sources

The Educational Loan Program of the Tuition Plan*-A Fixed-Rate Loan on Convenient Terms

The Concept-The Educational Loan Program of the Tuition Plan, a company of Chemical Banking Corporation is a fixed rate loan program designed to provide as much money as needed each academic year to pay for a student's course of study, depending on any local restrictions.

The loan may be used for any student for any education-related expense.

The loan may be used by any student enrolled in any preparatory school, college or graduate school in the United States.

The money may be borrowed by anyone willing to finance the education of that student.
The amount of money borrowed is based on the ability of the borrower to repay.

Low cost credit life insurance is available in most states and offered on an optional basis. The insurance will pay the amount of money not repaid, plus it covers all scheduled funds not yet disbursed.

The amount of money repaid each month is determined by the length of the educational program being financed. For the current interest rate for the Tuition Plan Loan Program, call 1-800-258-3640.

Finance charges are reduced because charges are only incurred when the funds are needed and used.

There are no origination or application fees or any other charges.

The school is not involved in the Tuition Plan Loan.

It's easy to apply for a Tuition Plan Loan or a Chemical ELC. Simply complete and mail the postage-paid application attached. Please indicate which unsecured loan option you would like to be considered for. If you desire Credit Life Insurance on the Tuition Plan Loan, please indicate so on the application. Further information will follow.

14 Non-governmental Loaning Sources

For quick processing please include some form of income verification. This includes a W-2 Form or Pay Statement and for self-employed applicants, the last two years' signed tax returns. If you have any questions regarding this or any other Educational Financing Group Plan, call toll-free (1-800-258-3640).

Chemical's Educational Financing Group offers the following programs:
Chemical Bank

* Federal Stafford Loans (subsidized and unsubsidized)
* Federal Supplemental Loans for Students
* Federal Plus Loans
* Alumni Advantage (Federal Loan Consolidation)
* Educational Line of Credit The Tuition Plan
* Educational Loan Program
* Educational Financing Manager

For information on any of these programs, please call toll-free 1-800-258-3640.

The following is from the Bank of Boston Alliance Education Loan Fact Sheet.

Bank Of Boston
Education Loan Department
P.O. Box 1296 99-26-08
Boston, Ma 02104

Introduction

The toughest part of higher education can be paying for it. That's why Bank of Boston developed the Alliance Education Loan.

For any students and families, an Alliance Loan is the simplest and most convenient way to finance a college education. Alliance may be your best choice if you simply want one loan each year for college. Or it may be an ideal supplement to other loans which you are already receiving. Either way, Alliance offers a number of advantages:

- Sizeable loan amounts of up to $20,000 per year ($80,000 cumulative maximum).
- Flexible interest-only payments while the student is in school.
- An easy-to-complete application and a fast loan approval process.
- A variety of long, easy-to-manage repayment terms.

WHO MAY APPLY

Any person in need of financial assistance to meet undergraduate or graduate school costs may apply. There are no maximum income limits or "needs" tests.

The student is always required to be one of the applicants on the loan and a signer on the promissory note. This way, the student begins to establish a credit history. Because many students are not sufficiently creditworthy to qualify for Alliance on their own, a parent, spouse or other individual is frequently a co-applicant and co-signer on the loan.

The student must be a degree candidate at a school approved by TERI, the guarantee agency for Alliance Loans. TERI also requires that at least one applicant be a U.S. citizen or Permanent Resident. Applicants need not be Massachusetts residents or attend college in Massachusetts.

LOAN AMOUNTS

The maximum Alliance Loan for one academic year is $20,000, and the minimum is $3,000. The maximum annual loan cannot exceed the student's total annual education costs minus any financial aid received. The school determines this "cost less aid" figure. Applicants attending schools with a tuition prepayment plan may borrow more than $20,000 per year. The cumulative maximum loan amount per student is $80,000. Loan proceeds must be used solely for educational purposes.

INTEREST

The Alliance Loan is a variable rate loan with an interest rate equal to the Bank of Boston's Base Rate plus two percent (2%). The Base Rate is the rate of the interest announced from time to time by the Bank at its head office as the Base Rate. Historically, it has closely tracked the Prime Rate in The Wall Street Journal.

REPAYMENT

You pay only monthly interest on the loan while the student is in school. The amount of interest due may fluctuate from month to month depending on changes in the Bank's Base Rate.

You may elect to make principal payments while the student is in school. There are no prepayment penalties.

Repayment of principal and interest begins within 60 days of the student's graduation or separation from school. At that time, you choose from a variety of repayment terms. The maximum term is 15 years. The amount of your monthly payment ($50 minimum) will be fixed, but the total number of payments may increase or decrease depending on changes in the Bank's Base Rate.

LOAN GUARANTOR

The Education Resources Institute (TERI), a non-profit corporation, is the guarantor for the Alliance Loan. TERI requires that a guarantee fee be paid by all Alliance borrowers. This fee is usually deducted from the loan amount before the funds are disbursed. However, you have the option to increase your loan to include the fee. The guarantee fee as of April 1,1989 is 4% of the loan amount. This fee affects the Annual Percentage Rate (APR) of the loan amount. Because Alliance is a variable rate loan, the APR is subject to increase after the loan is made.

LOAN EXAMPLES

The following chart is based on Bank of Boston's Base Rate (11.50%) as of April 1, 1989. Because the Alliance rate is equal to the Base Rate plus two percent, the interest rate for this chart is 13.50%. The chart assumes no change in the interest rate over the life of the loan.

Line 1 assumes you borrow $5000 in the student's freshman year and do not borrow again. Line 2 assumes you borrow $5000 in the freshman year and $5000 in the sophomore year and do not borrow again. Line 3 assumes you borrow $5000 in each of the student's freshman, sophomore, junior, but not the senior year. Line 4 assumes that you borrow $5000 in each of the four undergraduate years.

14 Non-governmental Loaning Sources

Monthly Principal and Interest Payments | Monthly Interest-Only Payments

Loan Amount	Year 1	Year 2	Year 3	Year 4	Yrs.5-20
1. $5000 for 1 year	$56.25	56.25	56.25	56.25	64.92
2. $5000 each year for 2 years	56.25	112.50	112.50	112.50	129.83
3. $5000 each year for 3 years	56.25	112.50	168.75	168.75	194.75
4. $5000 each year for 4 years	56.25	112.50	168.75	225.00	259.66

APR

*1. 14.18%
*2. 14.20%
*3. 14.23%
*4. 14.26%
* These rates are now lower

HOW TO APPLY
You should send the completed application to the financial aid office at

the student's school. There, the student's attendance will be verified and the cost of education less financial aid will be computed. The school will forward the application to Bank of Boston.

A credit decision will usually be made by the Bank within five business days of receipt of the completed application. Applicant One will be notified of the credit decision by mail. The school will also be notified of the decision. All subsequent correspondence will be sent to Applicant One.

WHEN TO APPLY
Bank of Boston accepts Alliance application at any time. Because each Alliance Loan fulfills only one year's education costs, you may wish to apply again each year to meet the student's new expenses. the same co-signers should apply each year if you wish to consolidate your billing statements. Previous Alliance borrowers will be sent a renewal application each year.

DISBURSAL OF FUNDS
Approved Alliance Loan applicants will be sent a promissory note by Bank of Boston. When the note is returned to the Bank, the disbursal process will begin. Loan funds will be disbursed directly to the school approximately one week prior to the school's tuition due date. If the school year is already under way, the loans will be sent to the school immediately.

The school should deduct from the Alliance Loan funds the amount necessary for the students's tuition, room, board and other fees. Any remaining funds may be returned to the student, depending on individual school policy. Borrowers should contact the school for further information.

BILLING
Bank of Boston will send a monthly statement to Applicant One. The statement will include the amount of the payment due and the due date as well as other information about the loan account.

It is the responsibility of the borrower to notify Bank of Boston when the student graduates, transfers schools or otherwise ceases to be enrolled.

14 Non-governmental Loaning Sources

OTHER SOURCES OF FINANCIAL AID

Government-Guaranteed Loan Programs
Applications for the Stafford Loan (FFELP), the Parent Loan (PLUS), and the Supplemental Loan to Students (SLS) are available at all Bank of Boston offices or by calling or writing the Bank.

Home Equity Credit Line
If you have a primary residence or vacation home in Massachusetts, New Hampshire or Rhode Island, a Bank of Boston Home Equity Credit Line is another flexible resource to meet education costs. This is a line of credit secured by the equity in your home that allows you to borrow money for almost any purpose, simply by writing a check. With a Home Equity Credit Line, there is no guarantee fee, and your loan interest may be fully tax deductible. You can choose among low variable or fixed rates and tailor your repayment plan to your specific needs. The variable interest rates range between 1% to 2% over Base Rate, depending on if you have a Bank of Boston personal deposit account and the deposit balances you maintain. One-time costs associated with placing the mortgage on your property (such as attorney or appraisal fees) may apply. Additional information and applications are available by calling the Bank.

INFORMATION
Please call Bank of Boston's Education Loan Department if you have any questions about completing your Alliance application, or if you would like additional information.

Bank of Boston
Education Loan Department
P.O.Box 1296 99-26-08
Boston, Ma 02104

1-(800)-637-6007
1-(617)-434-8970

Below is a reprint of a circular from The Educational Resources Institute, 330 Stuart Street, Suite 300, Boston, MA 02116. 1-800-255-TERI

Professional Educational Plan (PEP) Fact Sheet

TERI (The Educational Resources Institute)

Introduction

The Professional Education Plan(PEP) is a private, low cost loan plan designed to help undergraduate, graduate, and professional school students pay education costs. Through PEP, eligible students can borrow up to $20,000 a year to cover professional school costs. Interest rates are low; repayment terms are flexible, and there is no income limit or "needs test" to qualify. A special deferment option allows students to postpone payment of principal and interest while enrolled in school.

PEP is sponsored by The Education Resources Institute (TERI), a private, non-profit organization, and loans are available through participating lenders. Before you apply for a PEP loan, TERI encourages you to consider state and federal assistance programs, and to consult with your financial aid administrator at your school.

Eligibility

Any student enrolled at least half-time in a TERI approved program at a college or university in the United States may apply. The student must be credit-worthy or provide a credit-worthy co-borrower. At least one applicant must be U.S. citizen or a certified, permanent resident of the United States.

Approval

Loan approval is based on your credit history. In general, credit standards require a two-year minimum credit history and a demonstration of sufficient current income to meet current liabilities. In most cases, monthly installment expenses such as mortgage, auto and revolving payments can not exceed 40 percent of your net monthly income. Your lender will ask for income and employment verification. Also, the loan amount you apply for now will be included in the lender's debt-to-income analysis.

Keep in mind that if you have not established sufficient credit, you may still qualify for a PEP loan by obtaining a credit-worthy cosigner.

Loan Amounts

You may borrow $2,000 to $20,000 a year, not to exceed the cost of your education minus any other financial aid that you receive. Your school determines this amount and certifies your application. The total amount that you may borrow through the plan is $80,000. However, you are subject to an overall student loan debt limitation- including all educational loans such as Stafford Loan, Perkins Loan, HEAL- of $100,000.

Interest Rate

The interest rate is variable and will never exceed the lender's prime rate plus 2 percent. Check with participating lenders for specific details.

Fees

There are no application fees. The lender will collect a guarantee fee of 5 percent of the total loan amount, deducted directly from the loan check. This one-time fee, paid to TERI, allows you to borrow without pledging assets or collateral.

Deferment Option

You may defer, or postpone, payment of principal and interest for up to four and one-half years while you are in school. (During this time you may pay interest charges when billed.) If you choose to defer interest payment, any unpaid interest accrued while you are in school will be capitalized (added to your outstanding principal balance) six months after you graduate or leave school. You can avoid having interest capitalized by paying interest charges when billed.

Repayment

In most cases, your first payment of principal is due six months after you graduate. You have up to 20 years to repay, and there is no prepayment penalty. Once you start to repay, you will pay a fixed monthly amount. Any fluctuation in the interest rate will be reflected in the length of your

14 Non-governmental Loaning Sources

repayment period, not in your monthly amount.

For More Information

If you are interested in applying for a PEP loan, contact your financial aid office or call a participating lender. If you have question or would like more information about the Professional Education Plan, call TERI toll free at 1-800-255-TERI.

Participating Lenders

Baybanks, 858 Washington St, Dedham, MA 02026. (617)329-3700 x2080 or 1-800-332-TERI

Consumers Bank/Bank of New England Worcester, 40 Foster Street, Worcester, MA 01608. (508)791-7811

Below is a reprinting of a circular from Manufacturers Hanover, Educational Financing Group, 57 Regional Drive, Concord, NH 03301-9696

EDUCATIONAL FINANCING GROUP

AN INVESTMENT IN
EDUCATION PAYS
DIVIDENDS FOR LIFE
HERE ARE TWO EASY,
SURE WAYS TO FINANCE
THAT INVESTMENT

For many years Manufacturers Hanover Corporation- one of America's largest bank holding companies- has been committed to providing convenient, long-term financing to help families cope with the high cost of education.

Today, a year at a top school can cost $8,000, $10,000, or more. Even with scholarships, government loans, and other financial aid, many families cannot meet these costs without additional help.

Manufacturers Hanover Educational Financing Group offers government-backed unsecured loans, alternative loan programs, and budget programs to help meet this need.

Two of these options available from Manufacturers Hanover are our unsecured and non-governmental loan programs designed to assist parents and students in meeting the ever-rising costs of education:

--The Educational Line of Credit- a check activated line of credit based on a variable interest rate.

--The Educational Loan Program of the Tuition Plan - A fixed rate loan program based on convenient repayment terms, with the funds disbursed semester by semester.

Over the years, hundreds of thousands of students have been able to attend the educational institution of their choice through the convenient financing they received from the Manufacturers Hanover Educational Financing Group.

THE EDUCATIONAL LINE OF CREDIT (ELC) A CHECK-ACTIVATED VARIABLE INTEREST RATE LOAN PROGRAM

The Concept- The Educational Line of Credit (ELC) provides the borrower with a revolving line of credit. Using a book of personalized checks, the borrower pays school expenses by drawing against the line of credit.

The ELC is available at a competitive, variable interest rate. The Annual Percentage Rate (A.P.R.) is only 4.50% above the last highest Prime Rate as published in The Wall Street Journal and can change on a quarterly basis. This rate is competitive with other unsecured loans. For example, if the Prime Rate on November 15th is 10.00%, the A.P.R. on January 1st would be 14.50%.

The ELC may be used for tuition, room and board, transportation and any other education-related expenses - on any level from elementary through graduate or professional study.

The ELC may be used by parents, grandparents, guardians or others willing to finance the education of a student.

The school is not involved in the ELC because your agreement is a private contract between you and Manufacturers Hanover. The personalized checks are sent directly to the borrower, providing a confidential financial service.

Finance charges are low because checks are written and charges incurred only when the funds are needed and used. Most personal loans distribute funds once and charge interest on the full amount of the loan.

The annual expense for a Manufacturers Hanover ELC is low because the only costs for an ELC are principal and interest. There are no origination fees, application fees, closing costs, administrative or other charges. Some alternative financing programs charge an origination fee, while other types of loans, such as Home Equity Loans, require legal fees, a title search, points, mortgage tax and other closing costs which drive up the total amount of money borrowed.

Life insurance covering the entire unpaid balance is provided at no additional cost because Manufacturers Hanover wants to give the student and the borrower the peace of mind they deserve.

The limits to the ELC are a $5,000 minimum credit line ($2,500 for prep schools) and a $30,000 limit on the outstanding balance. The minimum check is $250.00. For any given academic year, funds which can be drawn upon may not exceed the total amount of the ELC divided by the number of years of study it covers.

The minimum amount repaid each month is determined by dividing the outstanding balance as of the last advance by 84, plus finance charges. (This term may be shorter on loans used for preparatory schools.) The minimum payment may be exceeded any time. Repayment begins 45 days after the funds are drawn from ELC.

If you have any questions regarding this call toll-free 1-800-258-3640.

THE EDUCATIONAL LOAN PROGRAM OF THE TUITION PLAN - A FIXED-RATE LOAN ON CONVENIENT TERMS

The concept - The Educational Loan Program of the Tuition Plan, a

14 Non-governmental Loaning Sources

company of Manufacturers Hanover, is a fixed rate loan program designed to provide as much money as needed each academic year to pay for a student's course of study, depending on any local restrictions.

The loan may be used for any student for any education-related expense,

The loan may be used by any student enrolled in any preparatory school, college or graduate school in the United States.

The money may be borrowed by anyone willing to finance the education of that student.

The amount of money borrowed is based on the ability of the borrower to repay.

Low cost credit life insurance is available in most states and offered on an optional basis. The insurance will pay the amount of money not repaid, plus it covers all scheduled funds not yet disbursed.

The amount of money repaid each month is determined by the length of the educational program being financed. For the current interest rate for the Tuition Plan Loan Program, call 1-800-258-3640.

Finance charges are reduced because charges are only incurred when the funds are needed and used.

There are no origination or application fees or any other charges.

The school is not involved in the Tuition Plan Loan.

1. The Tuition Plan, Donovan Street Extension, Concord, New Hampshire 03301; telephone 800-258-3640 or 603-228-1161 8888

2. Academic Management Services, 50 Vision Boulevard, East Providence, Rhode Island 02914; telephone 800-556-6684 or 401-431-1490

3. Alliance Education Loan,, c/o Bank of Boston, P.O. Box 1296, Mail Stop 99-26-11, Boston, Massachusetts 02105; telephone 617-434-8971

15 FOR THE MORE AFFLUENT

GIVE YOURSELF TIME TO PREPARE

It is wise, if possible, to give yourself time to accumulate college moneys or time to implement plans to accumulate funds.

If you have a stock that has appreciated in value, you might think of giving it to the future student. When it is sold the capital gains will be figured from the price of the stock at transfer time, not from the original purchase price.

BUYING A HOUSE OR CONDO

Some parents buy a house or condo in the town were their child is attending college. If the residence is large enough, the student can rent out a room. So besides supplying housing for their child, they can produce an income to help defray the mortgage payments. When the college education is completed, the house or condo is sold, ofttimes at a profit.

USING UNIFORM GIFTS TO MINORS

You can give to anyone each year $10,000 without a gift tax. You and your spouse together can give $20,000 each year. The giftee does not pay income tax on this money. Under the Uniform Gifts to Minors Act persons may make a gift to their child or grandchild etc., and register the gift in the name of a custodian for the child. This is provided for in the law. If the child is over 14 the dividends and capital gains can compound without tax or at a lower tax, normally, than the parents. If the child is under 14, the income or capital gain is credited to the parents, and is taxed accordingly. You can still claim your child as a deduction if you supply over 50 percent of the support.

You are not permitted, however, to use any of these funds for food, clothing, or other things you are legally obligated to provide your child. The funds are allowed to be used for a college education.

The role of gifts is central in preparing to pay for college. Gifts from

15 For The More Affluent

parents, grandparents, relatives, and friends are often a neglected subject. Paying for student's tuition and college costs is a major expense and gifts can be a direct use for this money. A gift is a change of capital that can have financial, legal, and tax considerations of major consequence to the donor and recipient. When correctly performed, a gift of money can have important effects on lowering income taxes and even estate taxes. Most significant, when correctly performed, gifts can create income to help pay for college.

Under the present tax code, a gift is not income. Therefore, a gift has no connection to the income of the donor and no tax effect for the recipient. Although a gift is income tax neutral, there is a gift tax. It is of major interest to the moneyed since it has been liberalized. One can give up to $10,000 a year to a person. A man and wife can give up to $20,000 to one individual. Gifts over these limits are subject to the gift tax. However, one can give 10 gifts of $10,000 each without being subject to the gift tax. Two exceptions to the $10,000 limitation are that one may give any amount to a dependent for medical expenses or to a student for tuition payments.

Anything annually over $10,000 is subject to a tax, i.e., a $12,000 gift, less the $10,000 exclusion, would leave $2,000 subject to tax. The tax would amount to $360. The tax commences at 18 percent with a maximum rate of 49 percent.

A major tax reform act in the early eighties allowed a credit of $192,800 to every American. No matter the gift tax, $360 or $7,200, it would not be paid but applied against the credit. If the tax exceeded the credit, the tax would be considered owed. The value of a gift must exceed $600,000 to use up the credit. When one surpasses the credit, one must pay the tax the following year. If the credit is never used up, the remainder may be applied to federal estate taxes.

The original cost of inherited property is not considered when this property is inherited and later sold. The value on the day of inheritance is considered the cost price. If shares were bought at $9 per share, and have a market price of $150 per share at the time of death, there is no tax on that appreciation. When the shares are sold, the gain will be measured from the new basis of $150 per share.

CHARITABLE REMAINDER TRUST

You can create what is known as a Charitable Remainder Unitrust. If you donate a set amount of money to a college and stipulate that a small percentage, along with earnings, each year, be paid into a custodial account created for your college bound child, then a college fund is being created for your child. The principal, at the end of a designated time, will go to the college. You have been able to take a tax deduction for a charitable donation to a college, and your child has a money fund to go to college. Contrary to other trusts, accumulated income is not taxed since the assets will eventually be contributed to charity. You should get help in setting up such a trust.

MINORS TRUST

The Minors trust is one of the most common trusts to establish. An attorney should be used in its creation as the trust rules must be spelled out in a legal document. The grantor establishes the trust by naming a child (or children) as recipient and installing the trustee with a gift of funds. Spare funds can be added in ensuing years. The trustee is charged with all the risk decisions, fulfilling the terms of the trust, and dividing income from the trust to the child or children. As a rule, the parent should not be the trustee, and the trust instrument should clearly state that the parent may not profit from the funds in any way, nor use them to fulfill any parental duty of support. Income from the assets will be taxed to the donor, if the donor exerts any control of the trust property.

The aim of this Minors trust is to move income from a high tax bracket to a low one and to prolong control over the money past the age of 18, the usual age of citizenry under the Uniform Gifts to Minors Act.

Income from the trust property can accrue in the trust and is assessed at the parent's tax rate until the child attains the age of 14. The trust is not taxed on the income it dispenses in the course of the year. The income is taxed at the child's rate after the child attains age 14.

This class of trust can dispense only interest income in the years before age 21. In the common college years the grantee would secure only interest income from the trust. There are the three possibilities when the recipient attains 21 years of age:

1st) The trust is terminated and grantee gets all the remaining assets.

2nd) The trust is terminated and the corpus reverts back to the grantors.

3rd) The corpus remains in trust for the grantee after 21, if he or she wants the trust intact.

In #3, the recipient has 60 days to withdraw the funds, or the capital is kept in the trust. This gives the trustee control of the funds beyond age 21.

Primarily the reason for the trust is to control the funds beyond the beneficiary's age 18. In a Uniform Gifts to Minors Act account, the custodian must terminate the account when the child turns 18 and release the funds to him or her. In a UGMA account, only certain types of property can be managed. In a trust, almost any kind of property may be managed.

Passbook accounts can be used as collateral. Banks and Thrifts will lend you back your own money. The bank will make money loaning you your own money. It will pay you X percent on your passbook account while it lends you money at a much higher rate, say twice the percentage they are paying you. Under the new tax code, earned interest will be taxable, but interest charges will not be deductible.

There are more instruments than the above, but I believe you would be better served to contact your CPA or Trust attorney.

16 SPECIAL FEDERAL SCHOLARSHIP

ROBERT C. BYRD HONORS SCHOLARSHIP PROGRAM -- EFFECTIVE FOR THE 1993-94 AWARD YEAR

The statute authorizes $10,000,000 for fiscal year 1993 and such amounts as are necessary for the next four fiscal years.

ELIGIBLE INSTITUTION OF HIGHER EDUCATION

The statute extends the Byrd Program institutional eligibility to include proprietary institutions of higher education and postsecondary vocational institutions as well as public and private nonprofit institutions of higher education.

PERIOD OF AWARD

The statute now provides that a state shall award a Byrd Scholarship to a scholar for a period of not more than 4 years of study at any institution of higher education.

ALLOCATION FORMULA

The statute modifies the allocation formula. The Secretary shall continue to allocate to each state an amount equal to $1,500 multiplied by the number of scholarships determined by the Secretary to be available to each state. The number of scholarships available to each state shall bear the same ratio to the number of scholarships made available to all states as the state's population ages 5 through 17 bears to the population ages 5 to 17 in all states. The Secretary shall determine the number of available scholarships by using the most recently available data, satisfactory to the Secretary, from the Bureau of the Census. The law also requires that a minimum of ten scholarships be made available to any state.

SCHOLARSHIP AMOUNT

The Byrd Scholarship award amount continues to be $1,500 for each selected scholar, except that the new statute requires that the total amount of financial aid awarded, including a Byrd Scholarship, cannot exceed the scholar's total cost of attendance at his or her postsecondary institution.

PACKAGING

Except as provided in section 471 of the HEA, which governs the amount of need, the receipt of a Byrd Scholarship shall not be counted for any needs test in connection with the awarding of any grant or the making of any loan under the HEA or any other provision of federal law relating to educational assistance.

ROBERT C. BYRD HONORS SCHOLARSHIP PROGRAM

This federally-funded program recognizes exceptionally able graduating high school students who show promise of continued excellence. The $1,500 scholarships are awarded on the basis of merit for the first year of study at an institution of higher education. A student submits the scholarship application to the financial aid office through his or her high school or GED training center. The applicant must be a graduate of a public or private secondary school (or have the equivalent of a certificate of graduation) and must have been admitted to an institution of higher education. High school GPA, college entrance examination scores and graduating class rank all play a part in the selection process. For more information on the Robert C. Byrd Honors Scholarship Program, contact counselors at the appropriate local high school or write the Robert C. Byrd Honors Scholarship Program, to the financial aid office at the college of your choice. Always include a stamped, self-addressed envelope.

17 MILITARY SERVICE AWARDS

MILITARY SCHOLARSHIPS

You can obtain funds for your education from the military before you go into service, while in service or after your discharge. The military will want something in return. It may not be as much as you think. If you anticipate a depressed economy it may be the way to go.

ROTC

There are two programs. In the regular four year program you qualify in your junior and senior years for a $100 a month stipend. In the 2, 3, 4, or 5 year scholarship program, which is very competitive, you receive tuition, fees, textbooks and $100 per month subsistence allowance. There are earlier deadlines on these programs. For more information write the following addresses, 1) Army ROTC, Ft. Monroe, VA 23651 2) AF ROTC, Office of Public Affairs, Maxwell AFB, AL 36112 3) Navy Recruiting Command, Code 314, 4015 Wilson Blvd., Arlington, VA 22203 4) Commandant of Marine Corps, Code MRRO-6 Hqs. USMC, Washington, DC 20308.

ACADEMIES

These are very competitive and take a congressional appointment besides. In addition to an education you receive living expense, clothing, medical care and an allowance. For more information write the following addresses, 1) Admissions Office, USMA, West Point, NY 10096 2) Director of Cadet Admissions, USAF Academy, CO 80840 3 (For the Navy and Marines) Superintendent, ATTN. Candidate Guidance, U.S. Naval Academy, Annapolis, MD 21402 -- non military service-- 4) Director of Admissions, U. S. Coast Guard Academy, New London, CT 06320 5) Admissions Office, U. S. Merchant Marine Academy, Kings Port, NY 11024.

ACTIVE DUTY

Obviously there are drawbacks to being on active duty in the military, but there are also great advantages for obtaining a college education at low

17 Military Service Awards

cost with practical experience. This applies to men and women.

While in service the military encourages off duty college work, and the service picks up 75% to 90% of the cost.

For more information ask your respective recruiter about the Army's Servicemen's Opportunity College, the Navy's Campus for Achievement, and the Air Force's Community college of the Air Force.

While on active duty you can be earning credit on your GI Bill. You can allocate up to $2,700 in monthly payments or in a lump sum to your education fund. The government will match your contribution 2 for 1. At the end of your enlistment you could have up to $2,700 plus $5,400 or $8,100 in your education fund.

However, this amount can be enlarged. If you enlist in the infantry you receive a large educational bonus. Or under special circumstances if you owe a government loan The Secretary of Defense may repay that loan each year you are in service at the rate of $1,500 or 33% of the outstanding balance, whichever is larger.

18 HEALTH EDUCATION PROGRAMS

HEALTH EDUCATION ASSISTANCE LOANS (HEAL)

You apply through your school or write directly to HEAL, Room 8-38, 5600 Fisher's Lane, Rockville, MD 20857 for this loan. Medical, Dental Osteopathic, Optometry, Podiatry, and Veterinary Medicine students may borrow $20,000 a year up to a total of $80,000. Administration, Pharmacy, Clinical Psychology, Public Health, and Chiropractic students can borrow $12,500 per year up to a limit of $50,000.

There is a floating interest rate on these loans which is 3.5% higher than the interest on 91 day Treasury Bill average. Interest does not have to be paid during periods of schooling or deferment. The interest does, however, keep accruing and is added to the loan balance. Deferments include periods of up to four years for internship and residency and for service in the Peace Corps, Armed Forces, ACTION or the National Health Service Corps.

Excluding deferment periods a borrower has up to 25 years to repay the loan. This could run close to retirement age. If you are in default on your loan repayments, the government will retain Medicare or Medicaid payments due you.

The lender of HEAL Loans are banks, S&Ls, credit unions, insurance companies, pension funds, state agencies and some schools that participate in the program.

Students attending a foreign medical school may not use the HEAL Program.

HEALTH PROFESSION STUDENT LOAN (HPSL)

These loans cover tuition plus $2,500 per year or the amount of the students need, whichever is less. They are for Medical, Dental, Osteopathic, Optometry, Podiatry, Pharmacy and Veterinary Medicine students. The student must show financial need. The interest charged is 9% and no interest is charged during schooling or periods of deferment.

You must apply through your school. All accredited schools in the U.S. and Puerto Rico are eligible. Students attending a foreign medical school are not eligible. If after graduation you practice in a shortage area (this will be explained below) the government will repay part of the loan.

A shortage area is in general a locale in which a particular health specialty is in greater demand than there is supply. The exact definition changes with each new appropriation bill. Whatever the definition, your request for aid is more likely to be looked upon favorably if you indicate your willingness to practice your profession in a shortage area.

Under the following conditions the loan will be canceled: 1) student's death or total disability, 2) the student fails to complete studies and is from a low-income or disadvantaged family. Since the low-income standard changes each year, please check.

If you practice your specialty in a shortage area for two years the government will cancel 60% of the principal and interest. An additional 25% will be canceled if you stay an additional year.

Repayment begins one year after the completion of your studies or deferment, and repayment can be spread over ten years. This loan can be consolidated with other loans. Contact the Division of Student Services, Bureau of Health Personnel Development and Service, 5600 Fisher's Lane, Rockville, MD 20857.

NATIONAL HEALTH SERVICE CORPS SCHOLARSHIPS (NHSCS)

Dentistry, Medicine, Optometry, Osteopathy, Pharmacy, Podiatry, and Veterinary Medicine majors are eligible for scholarships, and as the need arises so are majors in Nursing (Baccalaureate, Advanced Degrees, Community Health, Midwifery, and Psychiatric) and Nutrition. These scholarships cover all tuition and fees plus a monthly stipend. After graduation you are obligated for service. For more information write NHSC Scholarships, 5600 Fisher's Lane, Rockville, MD 20857, or phone 1-800-638-0824.

EXCEPTIONAL NEED SCHOLARSHIPS

Available for majors in Medicine, Dentistry, Optometry, Osteopathy, Pharmacy, Podiatry, and Veterinary Medicine. This scholarship covers all tuition as well as monthly stipend. The scholarship is good for one year only, but at completion of the year participants have priority for a NHSC Scholarship. You should apply through the school for this scholarship.

NURSING STUDENT LOAN PROGRAM

Students seeking the following types of nursing degrees (Associate, Diploma, Baccalaureate and Advanced Degree) are eligible, based on need, for loans up to $2,500 per year and $4,000 the final two years to a maximum of $13,000. The rate of interest charged is 6%. This program is available at practically all nursing schools and should be applied for through the school. Deferments may be made for up to 5 years for a full time course leading to a graduate degree in nursing or up to 3 years for service in the Peace Corps, military or Public Health Service.

Repayment begins 9 months after completing school or deferment and extends over 10 years.

The loan may be cancelled by death, permanent total disability, working full-time as a registered nurse in a public or nonprofit private agency, for service in a nursing shortage area. If the student is from a low-income, disadvantaged family and does not complete the course of study the government will repay the loan.

For more information write VA Health Profession Scholarship Program, DM&S (14N), 810 Vermont Avenue NW Washington, DC 20420 or contact the Division of Student Services, Bureau of Health Personnel Development and Service, 5600 Fisher's Lane, Rockville, MD 20857.

COMMISSIONED OFFICER STUDENT TRAINING EXTERN PROGRAM (COSTEP)

After having completed two years in Administration, Dentistry, Medicine, Nursing, Optometry, Osteopathy, Pharmacy, Podiatry, and Veterinary Medicine, Nutrition, Clinical Psychology, Public Health, Occupational Safety, Social Work, Occupational Therapy, Physical Therapy, or Chiropractic Medicine you can serve as an extern in the medical facilities of the Public Health Service during school breaks of from 31 to 120 days. You get lieutenants pay during your work period. However, this work and pay carries no obligation of future service. For more information write COSTEP, Room 4-35, 5600 Fisher's Lane, Rockville, MD 20857.

VA HEALTH PROFESSION SCHOLARSHIPS

Presently Baccalaureate and Advanced Degree Nursing Students are eligible for this scholarship. In the future it may expand to cover Dentists, Doctors and Osteopaths. The scholarship covers tuition and allows for a monthly stipend. It does carry an obligation to work in a VA Hospital after graduation.

The above health programs are for the purpose of funding students. The programs that follow are for the purpose of funding schools. However, some of this money may be unused and available for student aid so it pays to know they exist.

For Occupational and Physical Therapists there is the:

REHABILITATION TRAINING PROGRAM

It offers monthly stipends for trainees. You should refer to this as Program 84.129 (Rehabilitation Counseling, Physical and Occupational Therapy, Prosthetics-Orthotics, Speech Pathology, Audiology, Rehab and Services to the Blind and Deaf.) You can obtain more information about this program by writing Rehabilitation Services Administration, Office of Special Education and Rehabilitative Services, Washington, DC 20202.

There are two programs for Baccalaureate, Advanced Degree, and Midwifery Nursing. The first is called PROFESSIONAL NURSE TRAINEESHIPS. This pays all tuition and an annual stipend. The second program, NURSE PRACTITIONER TRAINEESHIPS, pays the same award, but preference is given to applicants living in Shortage Areas. For more information write Division of Nursing, Room 5C267, 5600 Fisher's Lane, Rockville, MD 20857.

For Advanced Degree Nursing there is NURSE FELLOWSHIPS (NRSA). You can get support up to 5 years for predoctoral study and up to 3 years for postdoctoral study. For more information write Division of Nursing, Room 5C26, 5600 Fisher's Lane, Rockville, MD 20857.

Two other graduate level programs are TRAINEESHIPS IN GRADUATE PROGRAMS OF HEALTH ADMINISTRATION and GRADUATE LEVEL PUBLIC HEALTH TRAINEESHIPS. The latter covers almost every graduate health field. Both pay tuition and an annual stipend. Write Division of Associated and Dental Health Professions, HRSA, 5600 Fisher's Lane, Rockville, MD 20857.

Three programs in the field of psychiatry are PSYCHIATRIC NURSING, MENTAL HEALTH - PSYCHOLOGY, and MENTAL HEALTH - SOCIOLOGY. These are for the fields Psychiatric Nursing, Clinical Psychology, and Social Work. These awards pay all tuition and an annual stipend. There is a service obligation when you complete the program. For further information contact, respectively, Psychiatric Nursing Education Branch, or Psychology Education Branch, or Social Work Education Branch - National Institute of Mental Health, 5600 Fisher's Lane, Rockville, MD 20857.

CHILD WELFARE TRAINING GRANTS are available for Social Work. For undergraduates the award is $1,000 per year; for graduates the award is larger. Refer to program 13.648 when contacting Children's Bureau, P.O. Box 1182, Washington, D.C. 20013.

For persons studying Occupational Safety, Program 13.263 OCCUPATIONAL SAFETY AND HEALTH TRAINING GRANTS may have awards for paraprofessionals, undergraduates, and graduates. Contact Center for Disease Control, Public Health Service, 5600 Fisher's Lane, Rockville, MD 20857.

NATIONAL HEALTH SERVICE CORPS LOAN REPAYMENT (NHSC Loan Repayment Program) These loans are provided for repayment of educational loans for participants who agree to serve an applicable period of time in a health manpower shortage area. The awards provide payments of up to $20,000 a year. Applicants must be enrolled as full-time students in an accredited health profession education institute; or possess a health professions degree. For more info. contact Division of Health Services Scholarships, Room 7-34, 5600 Fishers Lane, Rockville,

18 Health Education Programs

MD 20857. (301)443-3744

FINANCIAL ASSISTANCE FOR DISADVANTAGED HEALTH PROFESSIONS STUDENTS (FADHPS) Assistance is available for disadvantaged health professions students who have exceptional financial need for completion of a degree in medicine, osteopathic medicine, or dentistry. Ask your school for an application. Applications and information can be obtained from the Student and Institutional Support Branch, Division of Student Assistance, Room 8-34, Parklawn Bldg.,5600 Fishers Lane, Rockville, MD 20857. (301)443-1173.

19 MILITARY MEDICAL PROGRAMS

The military will pay for your medical education through the following programs:

UNIFORMED SERVICES UNIVERSITY OF THE HEALTH SERVICES This is the School of Medicine with 175 openings annually.

Student's receive lieutenant's pay plus payment for tuition and expenses. For more information contact, Admissions, USUHS, 4301 Jones Bridge Rd, Bethesda, MD 20814.

HEALTH PROFESSIONS SCHOLARSHIPS There are 5000 awards per year in Medicine and Osteopathy. Large monthly stipends and all college expenses. For more information contact, Assistant Secretary of Defense (Health Affairs), The Pentagon, Washington, D.C. 20301 and ask for a scholarship fact sheet.

ROTC NURSE PROGRAM (ARMY AND AF) Some nursing schools are affiliated with an Army or AF ROTC unit. Those associated with the Army offer about 50 two year scholarships per year plus tuition and $100 per month. The AF pays $100 per month, but for more information write, Army ROTC, Ft. Monroe, VA 23651 or AF ROTC, Office of Public Affairs, Maxwell AFB, AL 36112.

20 MINORITY PROGRAMS

MINORITY PARTICIPATION IN GRADUATE PROGRAMS. Grants are provided to institutions that provide direct fellowship aid to minority graduate students who are accepted to the institution. Ask your institution for more information

INDIAN HEALTH SERVICE EDUCATIONAL LOAN REPAYMENT (IHS Loan Repayment Program) This program is provided for repayment of loan that were incurred for health professions educational expenses. Contact, Health Manpower Support Branch, IHS, Room 9A-22, Parklawn Bldg, 5600 Fishers Lane, Rockville, MD 20857. (301)443-4242.

INDIAN/ESKIMO/ALEUT

HIGHER EDUCATION ASSISTANCE PROGRAM. Need based scholarship and loan for undergraduate and graduate. Contact, Indian Education Resource Center, Box 1788, Albuquerque, NM 87103.

INDIAN FELLOWSHIP PROGRAM. Programs in business, engineering, and natural resources for undergraduates. Graduate programs in law, education, medicine. Tuition and stipend. Application date is September. Contact, OIE Fellowship Program, FOB-6, Dept. of Education, Washington, DC 20202.

INDIAN HEALTH SERVICE SCHOLARSHIPS. Allied health fields including pharmacy and nursing. Two subprograms 1) Preparatory Scholarship Program. Two years. Purpose is to assist Indians in successfully enrolling in health profession school. Tuition plus stipend. No service obligation. 2)Health Professions Scholarship Program. Open to all, but Indians receive priority. Tuition and stipend. Service obligation. Contact, Indian Health Service, Room 6A-29, 3600 Fishers Lane, Rockville, MD 20857.

ALL MINORITIES

MINORITY ACCESS THE RESEARCH CAREERS. Schools with a substantial minority student body are funded. Awards for juniors, seniors, and grads. Pays tuition and expenses. For participating school write, Director, MARC Program, NIGMS, Westwood Bldg, Room 9A-18, Bethesda, MD 20205.

LEGAL TRAINING FOR THE DISADVANTAGED. Helps students train for the legal profession. Trainees selected to match activities that are funded. For the list of activities contact, Institutional and State Incentive Programs, Dept. of Education, 400 Maryland Ave, SW, Washington, DC 20202.

GRADUATE STUDY IN SCIENCES, MATHEMATICS AND ENGINEERING. Award is $6,900 per year. Contact National Science Foundation, Washington, DC 20550.

21 VETERANS PROGRAMS

VETERANS EDUCATION OUTREACH PROGRAM (VEOP) Accredited institutions can receive funds for veterans that attend. For more information on what schools participate in this program contact the Dept. of Education, Parklawn Bldg, 5600 Fishers Lane, Rockville, MD 20857.

POST-VIETNAM ERA VETERANS' EDUCATIONAL ASSISTANCE This program enables veterans to pursue educational, professional, or vocational objectives. An application form (VA Form 22-1990) may be obtained from any VA office or Regional Office.

VETERANS EDUCATIONAL ASSISTANCE This program assists veterans in attaining an educational, professional, or vocational objective at an approved institution. An application form (VA Form 22-1990v) may be obtained from any VA office or Regional office.

VA DEPENDENTS EDUCATIONAL ASSISTANCE The wives and children of veterans who died or were totally disabled as the result of service in the armed services as well as dependents of POWs and MIAs are eligible for awards. You should contact your nearest VA office.

22 MORE UNDERGRADUATE SOURCES

SUMMER EMPLOYMENT AND SUMMER INTERN Contact your nearest Federal Job Information Center. Almost 40,000 jobs per summer are available on a competitive basis.

COOPERATIVE EDUCATION Jobs with the Federal Government. Almost 16,000 positions. Students earn about $6,800 per year to start. Over 800 colleges participate. Contact the college financial aid officer.

JUNIOR FELLOWSHIPS Upper 10% of high school graduates are eligible. Opportunity to work in federal agencies during all college breaks. 5000 vacancies. Contact the college financial aid officer.

MARINE SCIENCES Sea Grant Program and Sea Grant Fellowship Program. Both grad and undergraduate. This program is funded through sea grant colleges. School list can be obtained from, Office of Sea Grants, 6010 Executive Blvd., Rockville, MD 20852.

MATH AND SCIENCE TEACHERS For college juniors. Award is a scholarship. Program still being developed. Contact Public Affairs, Dept. of Education, 400 Maryland Ave., SW, Washington, D.C. 20202.

LIBRARIANSHIP Library Career Training Program. Studies for paraprofessional and professional. Funded schools select the trainees and scholars. For a list of schools, contact the Office of Libraries and Learning Technologies, Dept. of Education, 400 Maryland Ave, SW, Washington, D.C. 20202.

MERCHANT MARINE Subsistence allowance of $100 per month for many students at TX, CA, ME, MS, SUNY, and Great Lakes Maritime Academies. There is no service obligation. Contact Academies Program Officer, Maritime Administration, Washington, D.C. 20230.

PUBLIC SERVICE Harry S. Truman Scholarship Foundation. 100 plus awards. $5,000 per year. Top students. Award begins your junior year and can extend for two graduate years. Award nominated by college. Each state has at least one award. Contact Truman Scholarship Foundation, 712 Jackson Place, NW, Washington, D.C. 20006.

SPECIAL EDUCATION Career preparation training at undergraduate and graduate levels. The training is funded through the school. Contact Personnel Preparation, Office of Special Education, Dept. of Education, Washington, D.C. 20202.

BILINGUAL EDUCATION Programs in languages and teacher preparation. Yearly stipend. Call 1-800-336-4560. In VA call 1-800-522-0710. Ask for information on participating schools and languages offered.

CONGRESSIONAL TEACHER'S AWARD OR PAUL DOUGLAS SCHOLARSHIP PROGRAM. An eligible scholar may receive an award of up to $5,000 for each academic year, not to exceed 4 years, provided he or she maintains a 3.0 GPA on a 4.0-point scale. Students who graduated in the top 10% of their high school class, or received a comparable score on their GED examination, & who are enrolled full-time at a school offering an approved teacher education program may qualify for this scholarship. High school or college GPA, financial need, a writing sample & a teacher recommendation all play a part in the selection process. Students failing to teach at least 2 years for each year's scholarship (or 1 year per scholarship year if teaching in certain schools) must repay the uncancelled scholarships plus interest. The interest rate is set each July 1 by the federal government & may vary. For applications and other information, students should contact the financial aid office of the college they plan to attend.
1993-94 Award Year

AUTHORIZATION OF FUNDS

The statute authorizes $26,000,000 for fiscal year 1993 and such sums as may be necessary for each of the four succeeding fiscal years to carry out the Paul Douglas Teacher Scholarship Program.

NUMBER OF SCHOLARS

The statute deletes the 10,000 limit on the number of individuals who may receive a Douglas scholarship.

ALLOCATION FORMULA

The statute amends the current allocation formula. It substitutes a formula that allocates funds to a state on the basis of state's school-age population compared to the school-age population in all states, as determined by using the most recently available data from the Bureau of the Census.

CHANGES TO A STATE'S APPLICATION TO PARTICIPATE

The statute changes the state application requirements in the following ways:

1. To administer the program, a state may now designate the state agency administering the SSIG Program, the state guaranty agency, or another appropriate state agency approved by the Secretary.

2. A state must now describe how it will inform recipients of the current and projected teacher shortages and surpluses within the state.

3. In addition to making specific efforts to attract students from low-income backgrounds or who express a willingness or desire to teach in institutions having less than average academic results or serving large numbers of economically disadvantaged students, a state now must assure the Secretary that it will make special efforts to attract into the program (a) ethnic and racial minority students; (b) individuals with disabilities; (c) women and minority who show interest in pursuing teaching careers in mathematics and science; (d) other individuals from groups historically underrepresented in teaching; and (e) individuals who express a desire to teach in rural and urban schools.

4. The statute deletes the requirement that states must provide assurances that scholarships will be awarded without regard to sex, race, handicapping condition, creed, or economic background. (However, all pertinent civil rights laws remain applicable.)

5. The statute modifies the state assurance concerning the agreement between the scholar and the state agency by:

a. Deleting the option for a scholar to fulfill his or her teaching obligation by teaching in a public or private nonprofit education program within a state; and

b. Adding an option for a scholar to fulfill his or her teaching obligation by teaching, on a full-time basis, in a private, nonprofit institution, teaching children with disabilities or with limited English proficiency.

SELECTION CRITERIA AND PROCEDURES

The statute now requires the state educational agency, working in cooperation with the state higher education agency, to establish the selection criteria to select scholars.

The statute also requires that the state educational and state higher education agencies provide special consideration in the selection of scholarship recipients to individuals who (a) intend to teach or provide related services to students with disabilities; (b) intend to teach limited English proficient student; (c) intend to teach preschool-age children; (d) intend to teach in schools servicing inner city or rural or geographically isolated areas as defined by the Secretary; (e) intend to teach in curricular areas or geographic areas where there are demonstrated shortages of qualified teacher; or (f) are from disadvantaged backgrounds, including racial and ethnic minorities and individuals with disabilities and, as such, are underrepresented in the teaching profession or in the curricular areas in which they are preparing to teach. The statute also provides that the Secretary may waive this special consideration for no more than 25 percent of all individuals receiving a Douglas Scholarship in an award year.

EVALUATION

The Secretary shall conduct an evaluation of the program, and the statute authorizes the use of up to $1,000,000 from the program's appropriations over five fiscal years for this purpose. The statute also requires the Secretary to prepare and submit interim reports and a final report that is due to the President and Congress on or before January 1, 1997.

TEACHER SHORTAGE AREAS

For loans to new borrowers disbursed initially after July 1, 1993, the statute deletes "the teacher shortage are deferment under section 428 of the Guaranteed Student Loan (GSL) programs (renamed the Federal Family Education Loans) and the requirements for establishing teacher shortage areas." The statute now provides that teacher shortage areas be established solely under the Douglas Program. When establishing areas, the Secretary must give special consideration to areas in which emergency teacher certifications are being used to correct teacher shortages and to states that have retirement laws permitting early retirement.

NATIONAL EARLY INTERVENTION SCHOLARSHIP AND PARTNERSHIP PROGRAM EFFECTIVE FOR THE 1993-94 AWARD YEAR

AUTHORIZATION OF FUNDS

The statute authorizes $200,000,000 for fiscal year 1993 and such amounts as might be necessary for the four succeeding fiscal years for this new program. However, no amount may be expended under this program in any fiscal year in which the amount appropriated for the State Student Incentive Grant Program does not exceed $60,000,000. The Secretary will initiate this new program only if funds are appropriated by the Congress.

STATE ELIGIBILITY AND PLAN

To qualify for this program, a state must submit to the Secretary for approval a state plan for carrying out the activities of both a scholarship component and an early intervention component under the program. The state must also describe how it will provide funds for the program.

STATE MATCHING FUNDS

In its plan, a state must demonstrate to the Secretary that it will provide from state, local, or private funds at least one-half of the program costs and describe how those funds will be paid. All funds expended under this program supplement, and not supplant, funds expended for existing state and local programs. A state may match the federal funds by means of the following:

(1) Grants paid to students under the program from state, local, or private funds;

(2) Tuition, fees, and room and board waived or reduced for recipients under this program; and

(3) Funds expended on documented, targeted, long-term monitoring and counseling provided by volunteers or paid staff of non-school organizations.

EARLY INTERVENTION COMPONENT

A state must demonstrate to the satisfaction of the Secretary that the state will provide comprehensive monitoring, counseling, outreach, and supportive services, including postsecondary financial aid counseling, to students in preschool through grade 12.

ALLOWABLE PROVIDERS

Early intervention activities may be provided by service providers such as community-based organizations, schools, institutions of higher education, public and private agencies, nonprofit and philanthropic organizations, businesses, and other organizations the Secretary deems appropriate.

PERMISSIBLE ACTIVITIES

Examples of permissible early intervention activities under the program include the following:

1. Providing eligible students in preschool through grade 12 with a continuing system of monitoring and advising that is coordinated with the federal and state community service initiatives and may include such support services as after-school and summer-school tutoring, assistance in obtaining summer jobs, career monitoring, and academic counseling;

2. Requiring each participating student to enter into an agreement under which he or she agrees to achieve certain academic milestones, such as completing a prescribed set of courses and maintaining satisfactory

academic progress, in exchange for receiving tuition assistance for a time period established by each state;

3. Providing activities designed to ensure high school completion and college enrollment of at-risk children; and

4. Providing prefreshman summer programs that (a) are at institutions of higher education with programs of academic-year supportive services for disadvantaged students; (b) assure the participation of disadvantaged students; (c) provide summer instruction in remedial, developmental or supportive courses, or summer services such as counseling, tutoring or orientation; (d) provide grant aid to cover prefreshman summer costs; and (e) assure that participating eligible students will receive financial aid during each academic year they are enrolled at the participating institution after the prefreshman summer.

PRIORITY STUDENTS

The state must treat as priority students, for its early intervention component, any student in preschool through 12 who is eligible (1) to be counted as attending a Chapter I school; (2) for the National School Lunch Program; or (3) for Aid to Families with Dependent Children assistance.

SCHOLARSHIP COMPONENT

Each participating state must establish or maintain a financial assistance program for the students in this program. The Secretary shall encourage the state to ensure that the tuition assistance under this program is available for use at any institution of higher education.

GRANT AWARDS

Each state must set the maximum amount a participating student may receive under this program. The minimum amount of the grant shall not be less than the lesser of (1) 75 percent of the average cost of attendance for an in-state student enrolled in a 4-year program of instruction at public institutions of higher education in the state, as determined by regulations established by the Secretary; or (2) the maximum Federal Pell Grant for that fiscal year.

RELATION TO OTHER FINANCIAL ASSISTANCE

Tuition assistance under this program is not to be considered for the purpose of awarding Title IV aid, except that the total Title IV aid awarded to the student cannot exceed the student's cost of attendance.

ELIGIBLE STUDENTS

A student eligible for scholarship assistance must:

(1) be less than 22 years old at the time of the first grant award;

(2) receive a high school diploma or a certificate of high school equivalence on or after January 1, 1993;

(3) be enrolled or accepted for enrollment at an institution of higher education that is located within the state, except that a state may offer grant portability for recipients who attend institutions outside the state; and

(4) have participated in the state early intervention component under this program.

The Secretary is required to ensure that each state place a priority on awarding scholarships to Federal Pell Grant recipients.

EVALUATION

Each participating state must conduct an evaluation of its early intervention on a biannual basis according to standards and requirements established by the Secretary. Each state is required to submit a copy of the evaluation to the Secretary, who will use the state evaluations to prepare a required biannual report to the Congress.

PRESIDENTIAL ACCESS SCHOLARSHIPS (PAS) EFFECTIVE FOR THE 1993-94 AWARD YEAR

AUTHORIZATION OF FUNDS

The statute authorizes $200,000,000 for fiscal year 1993 and such amounts as might be necessary for the four succeeding fiscal years for this new program. However, no funds may be expended on this program for a fiscal year unless the funds are appropriated for the Federal Pell Grant Program for that year. The Secretary will initiate this new program only if funds are appropriated by the Congress.

AWARD AMOUNT

Provided sufficient appropriations are available, each student receiving a Presidential Access Scholarship (PAS) is eligible to receive up to the greater of $400 or 25 percent of his or her Federal Pell Grant, except that a PAS added to the Federal Pell Grant and other available student financial assistance cannot exceed the student's cost of attendance.

PERIOD OF AWARD

A PAS recipient may receive the scholarship for not more than 4 academic years, or 5 academic years if the recipient is enrolled in an undergraduate course of study that requires attendance for the full-time equivalent of 5 academic years.

STUDENT ELIGIBILITY REQUIREMENTS

Initial award: The Secretary may award an initial PAS to a student who:

(1) Applies to the Secretary for a scholarship;

(2) Is eligible to receive a Federal Pell Grant;

(3) Within 3 years of receiving his or her high school diploma or General Education Development certificate, is enrolled or accepted for enrollment in a degree or certificate program of at least 2 years in length at any institution of higher education.

(4) Has demonstrated the potential for success in postsecondary education by taking a specified college preparatory program;

(5) Has earned a combined 2.5 grade point average or higher on a 4.0 scale in the final 2 years of high school; and

(6) Has either (a) graduated in the top 10 percent of his or her high school graduating class; or (b) participated for at least 36 months in an early intervention program. The Secretary may waive the second part of this requirement if an early intervention program was not available in the area in which the student resides or the student was unable to participate in an early intervention program where the student resides.

CONTINUATION AWARD

To continue to receive a PAS, a scholar must continue to be eligible for a Federal Pell Grant in the same academic year in which he or she receives a PAS, including maintaining satisfactory academic progress.

APPLICATION PROCESS

A student must apply to the Secretary to be considered for an initial award. As the statute requires that the student must also be eligible to receive a Federal Pell Grant, a student must apply for a Federal Pell Grant.

STATE EDUCATIONAL AGENCY AGREEMENT

Before any eligible student may receive a PAS, the state education agency (SEA) in the student's state of legal residence must enter into a written agreement with the Secretary concerning certain PAS Program requirements, the availability of certain college preparatory secondary coursework, and other procedures necessary to implement the PAS Program.

23 GRADUATE AWARDS

ENGINEERING AND SCIENCES Stipends and tuition for Ph.D. students. Supported by Department of Energy and Defense. No service obligation. Contact Energy: University Programs, Oak Ridge Associated Universities, P.O. Box 117, Oak Ridge, TN 37830 or Navy: ASEE, 11 Dupont Circle, Suite 200, Washington, D.C. 20036 or USAF: Office of Scientific Research, Bolling AFB, Washington D.C. 20332.

INTERNATIONAL EDUCATION National Resource Center and Fellowship Programs. Studies in languages and locales. 800 Awards. Awards are through the schools, write Office of International Education, Department of Education, 400 Maryland Ave, SW, Washington, D.C. 20202.

GRADUATE FIELDS Graduate and Professional Study. There are two subprograms. 1) Graduate and Professional Opportunity Fellowships. Purpose of awards is to increase participation of under-represented groups. 2) Public Service Education Fellowships. Fellows are selected by schools. For school list write, Institutional and State Incentive Programs, Department of Education, 400 Maryland Ave, SW, Washington, D.C. 20202.

INTERNATIONAL EXCHANGE Fullbright Scholarships. Live and study abroad for one academic year Write IIE, 809 UN Plaza, New York, NY 10017.

SCIENCE Graduate Fellowships. Write, National Science Foundation, Washington, D.C. 20550.

MARINE SCIENCES Sea grant Program and Sea Grant Fellowship Program. Both grad and undergraduate. This program funded through sea grant colleges. School list can be obtained from, Office of Sea Grants, 6010 Executive Blvd., Rockville, MD 20852.

PUBLIC SERVICE Harry S. Truman Scholarship Foundation. 100 plus awards. $5,000 per year. Top students. Award begins your junior year and can extend for two graduate years. Awardees nominated by college. Each state has at least one award. Contact Truman Scholarship Foundation, 712 Jackson Place, NW, Washington, D.C. 20006.

SPECIAL EDUCATION Career preparation training at undergraduate and graduate levels. The training is funded through the school. Contact Personnel Preparation, Office of Special Education, Dept. of Education, Washington, D.C. 20202.

24 POTPOURRI

STUDENTS WITH A FIRST BACCALAUREATE OR PROFESSIONAL DEGREE

A student is eligible for assistance under the FFEL, FWS, Federal Direct Loan, or Federal Perkins Loan programs though the student has previously received a baccalaureate or professional degree.

INCARCERATED STUDENTS

Incarcerated students should check with the financial aid office of the college they will be enrolled in so as to find out more about the Pell Grant.

Since incarcerated students cannot enter into a contract and thus, could not sign the required promissory note for the Perkins Loan, they are not eligible for the loans.

Incarcerated students sometimes have difficulty obtaining copies of their Student Aid Reports. An exception may be made for filling in the mailing address in these cases. A tactic has been installed whereby aid administrators have incarcerated students' SARs mailed to the college rather than to the prison address.

The aid administrator (FAO) should have the incarcerated applicant fill out completely the application form, put in the college's address on the address line, and sign and date the form. The address to which these applications are sent changes yearly. The aid administrator should contact the federal processor for this data.

The aid administrator will enclose a cover letter explaining that the student is incarcerated. Then he or she mails such request to the federal processor. He or she should document in the college's files that the student was in fact incarcerated when the request was mailed.

CORRESPONDENCE COURSES (STUDENT ELIGIBILITY)

A student is not eligible to receive Title IV grants, loans, or work assistance for correspondence courses that are not part of an associate, bachelor, or graduate degree program.

CORRESPONDENCE COURSE STUDENTS

An institution offering a full range of correspondence courses is Regents College Degrees, Cultural Education Center, Albany, NY 12230 Ph 518-474-3703. Ask for their catalog of courses

Eligible correspondence course study is an undergraduate program requiring at least 12 hours of study a week.

Correspondence students are not considered at full-time cost because they are not full-time students. The need is based on the student's actual cost for tuition and fees for the program or the academic year.

Before the correspondence school can dispense any money from the campus based programs the first correspondence lesson must be submitted. A correspondence student is considered at most a half time student during their time of enrollment. However, only "tuition and fees, and, if required, books and supplies, travel, and room and board costs incurred specifically in fulfilling a required period of residential training may be included in his or her cost of attendance."

REGULAR AND CORRESPONDENCE STUDY TOGETHER

The number of credits a student is taking, both regular and correspondence courses, determines whether that student is considered a full-time student or not, and is subject to certain limitations.

If an eligible student, who is taking in addition to regular course work, correspondence work either from the institution in which he/she is enrolled or has a written agreement from another college, the correspondence work may be included in the resolution of the student's enrollment status. The work must apply toward the student's degree/certificate or must be remedial work taken by the student to help in her/his course of study. In addition, the correspondence study must be taken in the required period of time for regular course work. The number of credits hours of correspondence work included in the student's enrollment status must not exceed the amount of the student's regular course work.

TELECOMMUNICATIONS

If the financial aid administrator (FAA) determines, using his or her professional judgment that the telecommunications instruction results in a substantially reduced cost of attendance to the student, the FAA must reduce the student's eligibility for grants, loans, or work-study assistance.

The statute defines "telecommunications" as the use of television, audio, or computer transmission, including open broadcast, closed circuit, cable, microwave, satellite, audio conferencing, computer conferencing, or video cassettes or discs. The term does not include a course that is delivered using video cassette or disc recordings that is not delivered in person to other students of the institution.

RECEIVE CREDIT FOR EXPERIENCE/EMPLOYMENT

A college may assign special credits to students who have past employment and experience, but they do not meet the enrollment status criteria for the Pell Grant program.

CREDIT BY EXAMINATION

A student may get credits towards a degree/certificate and satisfy course standards by passing an examination in specific subject areas, but these credits cannot be counted in ascertaining the enrollment status and they cannot be included in meeting the minimum credit criteria for acceptable progress.

REPEATING A COURSE

A student who repeats a course because he/she failed it or wants to improve the grade in the course, may use the credits for the total number of credits as long as the student is earning adequate headway and the college is allowing the student to receive credit for the repeated course. If the student got an Incomplete in the course, then the completion of that course may not be included in the decision of enrollment status unless the student re-registers for the entire course.

CREDIT FOR COOPERATIVE EDUCATION WORK

This program looks more attractive to parents than to students. I side with the parents, but that only lets you know that I am a parent. One attractive facet in this time of uncertainty is that you are almost assured of a position with your training company upon graduation.

Actually the Federal Government is the largest employer with over 16,000 openings each year. The Federal Government is ubiquitous, not just in D.C. The job openings range from anthropology to zoology. Private industries participates also. About 1000 colleges participate.

You begin at entry level wage and get raises. Expect to earn between 6 to $8,000 a year for 1,000 hours work. Your job will match your course of study. Your understanding of your studies will be greatly enhanced. Check with your financial aid counselor to find who heads up this program in your school.

A student participating in a cooperative education program, receives Pell-Grant assistance if the student receives academic credit while enrolled in the program. For a student who has a job through the Cooperative Education Program, the cost of attendance will be the tuition and fees for the school year, an allowance for living expenses, and child care and/or handicap expenses, if applicable. The college determines the credit a student will receive by assessing the work done as equivalent to part of the academic course load.

TUITION AND FEES FOR JOB TRAINING PARTNERSHIP ACT (JTPA)

In a program conducted by an institution with JTPA, students may get Pell Grants as long as the program remains eligible. If the cost of attendance actually included tuition and fee charges the student may use the Pell Grant for these.

SUMMER SESSION ALLOWANCE

When the summer session is considered part of the school year and the student has not been issued all financial aid allocation for that year, a check may be given to the student upon request for the summer session. The total allocation cannot exceed the amount of the award for that school year. Title IV aid is not in other cases issued for the summer.

PROGRAM AWARD AFTER PART OF ELIGIBILITY HAS BEEN USED

A student is entitled to only one scheduled award per year. He/She is responsible for repayment of any amount that exceeds the planned grant. When a student transfers from one school to another and has not used up the award acquired at the first school, then the student is qualified for another award at the second school. If the student relocates from a school that has higher costs than the second school, then the financial aid counselor should adjust the student's award appropriately. If a student's last term has not ended prior to his/her enrolling in the first term at the second institution, the student may receive a grant from both schools for the overlapping period of time.

LOSS OF ELIGIBILITY FOR VIOLATION OF LOAN LIMITS

No student is eligible to receive Title IV assistance if an eligible institution determines that the student <u>fraudulently</u> borrowed in violation of annual loan limits in the same academic year or in excess of the aggregate maximum loan limits under the FFEL, Federal Direct Loan, or Federal Perkins Loan programs. If the institution determines that the student <u>inadvertently</u> borrowed in excess of the loan limits, the institution is required to allow the student to repay the amount borrowed in excess of the limits prior to certifying the student's eligibility for further Title IV assistance.

LESS THAN HALF TIME ATTENDANCE

Cost of attendance for this group of students includes only tuition and fees, and allowances for supplies, books, travel and dependent care. Nothing is permitted for room or board or personal care.

REMEDIAL COURSES

Besides regular college work these funds are available for not more than one year of remedial courses at a college. One year means 30 semester hours, 45 trimester hours or 900 clock hours. Remedial courses are noncredit, but they increase the ability of the student to complete a course of study leading to a certificate or a degree. Not charged against the one year is "English as a second language." Courses that are designed to prepare students with inadequate education to strive successfully in college level programs are called remedial courses. Besides the three campus-based programs, the PLUS/SLS loans are available to students taking remedial courses. These two loans are discussed elsewhere in the book.

MEMBERS OF RELIGIOUS ORDERS

For determination of eligibility of a Pell Grant or campus based awards the Secretary of Education deems that a member of a religious order (society, community, organization or agency) who follows a program of study at an school of higher learning has no financial need if the religious order:

1. promotes, as its primary purpose, the ideals and beliefs of a Supreme Being;

2. mandates that its members waive any monetary or other support materially beyond the support it provides;

3. directs the members to follow the course of study;

4. gives survival support to its members.

FINANCIAL AID TRANSCRIPT

If a student has attended another institution, the institution the student is applying to for a loan will not make any disbursements without receiving a financial aid transcript from the previous institute.

VERIFICATION OF IMMIGRATION STATUS

The HEA authorizes use of a data match with other agencies to verify that an applicant is an eligible noncitizen. A data match (otherwise known as primary confirmation) with the Immigration and Naturalization Service (INS) is currently in operation and meets the requirements of this provision.

For applicants whose eligible noncitizen status is not verified through the data match, an institution is required to transmit copies of the applicant's documentation of immigration status to INS for official verification. (This process, otherwise known as secondary confirmation, is also currently available to institutions.) The institution is prohibited from denying the applicant's eligibility for Title IV assistance on the basis of the applicant's immigration status while receipt of verification from INS is pending. At the same time, the new law prohibits the institution from disbursing Title IV assistance until the applicant's statements or documentation (or both) of immigration status are verified.

FOREIGN STUDENTS

The following is quoted from the IMMIGRATION HANDBOOK.

"F-1 Student
Another nonimmigrant visa requested often is the foreign student visa (F-1).

Student visas are processed abroad by the American consulate. Like other nonimmigrant, a prospective foreign student must prove to the consul that he or she has an unrelinquished domicile abroad. Applicants must demonstrate that they have been accepted for a full course* of study in a school or university accredited by the INS to accept foreign students. (Full course of study for undergraduate work at a college or university - at least 12 hours of instruction a week.) As part of their visa applications, the aliens must present the completed I-20 form issued to them by the accredited school.

Prospective students must also show that they have sufficient financial support to cover all costs for the planned years of study including living expenses. Applicants are required to submit evidence of their source of funds, such as Affidavits of Support, Form I-134, evidence of scholarship aid, bank statements or other verification of monetary assistance.

If the student visa is granted, the applicant must then be inspected and admitted at a port of entry by an immigration inspector. In recent regulations the INS tightened controls on foreign students. The new rules, which took effect on February 23, 1981, limit the time for which students are admitted to a specific period. The date their admission will expire is to be determined by the time it normally takes to complete their course of study as indicated on form I-20 of the school they will attend. Extensions of stay to remain in the United States will be considered by the INS on a case by case basis."

"To become a non-academic/vocational student in the United States you must be accepted by a school which the Immigration and Naturalization Service has approved for attendance by nonimmigrant students. The school will issue a student eligibility form to you the I-20MN. This form is presented to the American consular officer to obtain your visa and to the immigration officer when you arrive in the U.S. You may be allowed to work in the United States for practical training. Ask your foreign student advisor for details."

The following non-citizens are eligible to apply for college governmental aid in the same manner as a citizen: 1) U.S. national 2) U.S. permanent resident, and you have an Alien Registration Receipt Card (1-151 or 1-551) 3) Permanent resident of the Northern Mariana Islands 4) Permanent resident of the Trust Territory of Pacific Islands 5) Other eligible non-citizen -- that is, you have one of the following documents from the U.S. Immigration and Naturalization Service: a) Arrival-Departure Record (1-94) showing Refugee or Adjustment Applicant 6) An official statement showing you have been granted asylum in the U.S.

A refugee is one who is unwilling or unable to return to their country because of persecution or a well founded fear of persecution on the account of race, religion, nationality, membership in a political group, or political opinion.

You must submit appropriate documentation to the school to verify your citizenship status. Only U.S. citizens or National may obtain a FFELP to attend a school outside of the United States.

FOREIGN STUDY

If a student wishes to study overseas for a year or two, naturally they should get things arranged with their present school first. When they pick out the foreign school that they want to attend, they should check with the federal information number 1-800-4FED AID. They will have a current list of the schools participating in the various loan programs for foreign study.

STUDY ABROAD PROGRAMS

A statement that enrollment in a program of study abroad that is approved for credit by the home institution may be considered enrollment in the home institution for purposes of a student applying for federal student financial assistance.

In order to receive financial aid a student must be enrolled or accepted for enrollment in a degree program, certificate program, or other program leading to a recognized educational credential at an institution of higher learning that is an eligible institution. If a student is enrolled or accepted for enrollment in a program of study abroad and that school is approved for credit by the eligible institution at which the student is enrolled, then that student is eligible for financial aid, without regard as to whether the study abroad program is required as part of the student's degree program.

DISBURSEMENT TO BORROWERS ENROLLED IN STUDY-ABROAD PROGRAMS

The HEA has been amended to provide that loan proceeds for borrowers who are in a study-abroad program that is approved for credit by a home institution must, at the borrower's request, be disbursed directly to the borrower. Alternatively, at the borrower's request, the loan proceeds may be disbursed to the borrower's home institution if the borrower provides a power-of-attorney to an individual not affiliated with the institution to endorse the borrower's check or complete an EFT authorization. A lender should continue to disburse loan proceeds directly to students attending eligible foreign institutions.

PROPRIETARY SCHOOLS [STUDENT ASSISTANCE GENERAL PROVISIONS -- EFFECTIVE JULY 1, 1993]

ELIGIBLE PROGRAM

To qualify as a proprietary institution of higher education or postsecondary vocational institution, an institution must provide an eligible program. An eligible program is either 1) A program of at least 600 clock hours, 16 semester hours, or 24 quarter hours that a) Is offered during a period of at least 15 weeks, b) Provides training to prepare students for gainful employment in a recognized profession, and c) Admits students who have not completed the equivalent of an associate degree; or 2) A program of at least 300 clock hours, 8 semester hours, or 12 quarter hours that is offered during a minimum of 10 weeks and a) Is an undergraduate program requiring the equivalent of an associate degree for admission, or b) Is a graduate or professional program.

The Secretary (of Education) will develop regulations to determine the quality of programs that are longer than 300 clock hours but shorter than 600 clock hours. The regulations will specify that these programs must have verified completion and placement rates of 70 percent. After publication of those regulations, programs shorter than 600 clock hours but longer than 300 clock hours that satisfy those regulations and meet the requirements in the just-cited item 2 will be eligible for any Title IV program. Programs shorter than 600 clock hours but longer than 300 clock hours that satisfy those regulations will be eligible for the FFEL Program only, even though they do not meet the requirement in item 2.

PROGRAM INTEGRITY PROVISIONS, STATE POSTSECONDARY REVIEW PROGRAM

STATE DEVELOPED REVIEW STANDARDS

The Secretary will notify each state of the institutions in the state that meet one or more of the statutory review criteria and will provide the state with a copy of the audits of the affected institutions. The designated state entity will then be required to review these institutions in accordance with standards, in the following areas, developed in consultation with the institutions in the state:

(1) The availability and accuracy of student consumer information materials given to students and prospective students.

(2) Assurance that the institution has a method to determine a student's ability to complete successfully the course of study for which he or she has applied.

(3) Assurance that the institution maintains and enforces academic progress standards and maintains adequate student and other records.

(4) Compliance by the institution with health and safety standards.

(5) The financial and administrative capacity of the institution as appropriate to a specified scale of operations and the maintenance of adequate financial and other information necessary to determine the financial and administrative capacity of the institution.

(6) For institutions financially at risk, the adequacy of provisions to provide for the instruction of students and the availability of academic and financial aid records of students in the event the institution closes.

(7) If the stated objectives of the courses or programs of the institution are to prepare students for employment, the relationship between the program length and the reasonable salary a graduate of the program can expect to receive and the relationship of the courses or programs to providing the student with quality training and useful employment in recognized occupations in the state.

(8) Availability to students of relevant information on job opportunities and state licensure requirements.

(9) The appropriateness of the number of credit or clock hours required for the completion of programs or of the length of 600 hour classes.

(10) Assessing the actions of any owner, shareholder, or person exercising control over the institution that may adversely affect eligibility for the Title IV programs.

(11) The adequacy of procedures for investigation and resolution of student complaints.

(12) The appropriateness of advertising, promotion, and recruiting

practices.

(13) That the institution has a fair and equitable refund policy.

(14) The success of the program at the institution including completion, graduation, placement, and withdrawal rates, pass rates on state licensing exams, and student completion goals (including transfer to another institution, employment or military service).

(15) With respect to an institution that meets one or more of the statutory review criteria, the state shall contract with the appropriate accrediting agency or association or another peer review system with demonstrated competence in assessing programs to carry out a review or provide information regarding such agency's or association's assessment of the following: The quality and content of the institution's courses or programs of instruction, training, or study in relation to achieving the stated objectives for which the space, equipment, instructional materials, staff, and student support services (including student orientation, counseling and advisement) for providing education and training that meets such stated objectives.

These review standards must be developed in a manner consistent with the laws and constitution of the state and are subject to disapproval by the Secretary.

In addition to the institution identified by the Secretary as having met one or more of the statutory criteria that require state review, a state entity may, subject to the approval of the Secretary, review institutions for which the state has determined to meet these criteria based on more recent data than that used by the Department, and institutions that the state has reason to believe are engaged in fraudulent practices. If the Secretary does not approve or disapproves within 12 days a state request for review of additional institutions, the state entity may proceed to review the institutions as if the state request had been approved.

LOSS OF INSTITUTIONAL ELIGIBILITY

A state review entity may determine, based on its own findings or the findings of a Federal entity, that an institution of higher education is not eligible to participate in the Title IV programs. If the state entity finds that an institution does not meet one or more of the state-developed review standards, the state entity must notify the Secretary of its findings and the actions that the state has taken or plans to take in response to the findings within a time period prescribed by the Secretary in regulations. If the state entity determines that an institution of higher education is not eligible to participate in the Title IV programs, the state entity must notify the Secretary, who will immediately terminate the institution's participation.

If the Secretary takes or plans to take any action against an institution of higher education, including any action taken with respect to institutional audits, the Secretary will notify the designated state review entity within a time period to be prescribed in regulations. The Department also will promulgate regulations regarding procedural standards for the disapproval of institutions of higher education by state review entities.

CONSUMER COMPLAINTS

A state, in consultation with institutions of higher education in the state, will be required to establish procedures for receiving and responding to student complaints about institutions and maintain records of such complaints to determine their frequency and nature for specific institutions.

STANDARDS REQUIRED FOR ACCREDITING AGENCY APPROVAL

No accrediting agency may be determined by the Secretary to be a reliable authority as to the quality of education or training offered, unless it meets standards established by the Secretary. Such standards include appropriate measures of student achievement and require that: the agency's standards of accreditation assess the institution's (A) curricula; (B) faculty; (C) facilities, equipment, and supplies; (D) fiscal and administrative capacity as appropriate to the specified scale of operations; (E) student support services; (F) recruiting and admissions practices, academic calendars, catalogs, publications, grading and advertising;
(G) program length and tuition and fees in relation to the subject matter

taught and the objectives of the degrees of credentials offered; (H) measures of program length in clock hours or credit hours; (I) success with respect to student achievement in relation to its mission, including, as appropriate, consideration of course completion, State licensing examination, and job placement rates; (J) default rates in the student loan programs under Title IV of HEA, based on the most recent data provided by the Secretary; (K) records of student complaints received by, or available to, the agency; and (L) compliance with its program responsibilities under Title IV of the HEA, including any results of financial or compliance audits, program reviews, and such other information as the Secretary may provide to the agency.

INSTITUTIONAL REFUNDS

Each institution participating in any Title IV program is required to have a fair and equitable refund policy under which the institution refunds unearned tuition, fees, room and board, and other charges to a student who received Title IV assistance (including Federal PLUS loans received on the student's behalf), in the case of a student who does not register for the period of attendance for which assistance was intended or withdraws or otherwise fails to complete the period of enrollment for which assistance was provided. This statutory requirement is somewhat similar to the regulatory requirement for a fair and equitable refund policy that was previously applicable to the FFEL Program only.

The HEA defines a "fair and equitable refund policy" as a policy that provides for a refund in an amount of at least the largest of the amounts provided under:

1. The requirements of applicable state law;

2. The specific refund requirements established by the institution's nationally recognized accrediting agency and approved by the Secretary; or

3. The prorated refund calculation as defined by the HEA. The HEA specifies that the prorated refund calculation does not apply to the institution's refund policy for any student whose date of withdrawal is after the 60 percent point in time in the period of enrollment for which the

student has been charged.

The term "prorated refund" is defined as a refund by the institution to a student who is attending the institution for the first time, of not less than that portion of tuition, fees, room and board, and any other charges assessed the student by the institution equal to the portion of the period of enrollment for which the student has been charged that remains on the last recorded day of attendance by the student, rounded downward to the nearest 10 percent of that period, less any unpaid charges owed by the student for the period of enrollment for which the student has been charged, and less a reasonable administra- tive fee not to exceed the lesser of 5 percent of the tuition, fees, room and board, and other charges assessed the student, or $100.

The term "the portion of the period of enrollment for which the student has been charged that remains" is determined:

For a program that is measured in credit hours, by dividing the total number of weeks that make up the period of enrollment for which the student has been charged, into the number of weeks remaining in that period as of the last recorded day of attendance by the student;

For a program that is measured in clock hours, by dividing the total number of clock hours that make up the period of enrollment for which the student has been charged, into the number of clock hours remaining to be completed by the student in that period as of the last recorded day of attendance by the student; and

For a correspondence program, by dividing the total number of lessons that make up the period of enrollment for which the student has been charged, into the total number of such lessons not submitted by the student.

STUDENT ASSISTANCE GENERAL PROVISIONS - CAMPUS SECURITY DISCLOSURES

The new laws add to the list of crime statistics that an institution must collect and require an institution to disclose additional information concerning campus programs to prevent sexual assault and mandate adoption of procedures for a victim to follow when a sex offense has occurred.

Effective August 1, 1992, each institution must collect statistics concerning the occurrence of forcible or non-forcible sex offenses on campus; previously, under the Student Right-to-Know and Campus Security Act, an institution was required to collect and disclose statistics concerning rape only. The institution must use the definitions of a forcible or non-forcible sex offense used in the Federal Bureau of Investigation's Uniform Crime Reporting System, as amended by the Hate Crime Statistics Act. These data must be collected from August 1, 1992 through December 31, 1992 and each calendar year thereafter. For the annual security report that the institution must disclose on September 1, 1993, the institution must disclose statistics concerning rape for the period August 1, 1991 through July 31, 1992, and statistics concerning forcible or non-forcible sex offenses for the period August 1, 1992 through December 31, 1992; the institution must also disclose in that report data reasonably available to the institution from campus and law enforcement authorities concerning forcible or non-forcible sex offenses for the period August 1, 1991 through August 1, 1992.

Effective July 1, 1993, the institution must have in place the following campus sexual-assault programs. These programs are established to prevent sex offenses, and the procedures must be explained in the annual security report provided by institutions and made available to current and prospective students and staff beginning September 1, 1993 and each year thereafter. These programs contain the following: 1. Education programs to promote the awareness of rape, acquaintance rape, and other sex offenses; 2. Possible consequences for rape, acquaintance rape, or other sex offenses (forcible or non-forcible) following an on-campus disciplinary procedure; 3. Procedures students should follow if a sex offense occurs, including who should be contacted, the importance of preserving evidence as may be necessary to the proof of criminal sexual assault, and to whom the alleged offense should be reported; 4. Procedures for on-campus disciplinary action in cases of alleged sexual assault that shall include a clear statement that: a. The accuser and the accused are entitled to the same opportunities to have others present during a campus disciplinary proceeding; and b. Both the accuser and the accused shall be informed of the outcome of any campus disciplinary proceeding brought alleging a sexual assault; 5. Informing students of their options to notify proper law enforcement authorities, including on-campus and local police, and the option to be assisted by campus authorities in notifying these authorities, if the student chooses to do so; 6. Notifying students of existing counseling, mental health or student services for victims of sexual assault, both on campus and in the community; and 7. Notifying students of options for, and available assistance in, changing academic and living situations after an alleged sexual assault incident if requested by the victim and if these changes are reasonably available.

In the institution's report for September 1, 1994, the institution must disclose the statistics described for August 1, 1991 through December 31, 1992 and 1993.

In the institution's report for September 1, 1995 and each succeeding year, the institution must disclose statistics concerning criminal offenses for the three calendar years (January 1 through December 31) preceding the year in which the report is made.

Public Law 102-325 amends the Family Educational Rights and Privacy Act (FERPA), also known as the Buckley Amendment; Public Law 102-325 eliminates prior FERPA restrictions on the disclosure of records that are created and maintained by campus law enforcement units for law enforcement purposes. This change became effective on July 23, 1992; the Department will issue a Notice of Proposed Rule-making to implement this statute. In the interim, if an institution has questions about this change or FERPA, the institution should contact the:

>   Family Policy Compliance Office
>   U.S. Department of Education
>   400 Maryland Avenue, SW
>   Washington, DC 20202-4605
>   Telephone Number: (202) 732-1807

COMPUTERIZED SCHOLARSHIP LOCATOR SERVICE

Student College Aid maintains a tie with a computer service that maintains a scholarship foundation data bank. A computer is a fast and economical method to find awards that match award characteristics to personal characteristics. An information dataform is sent to users. The answers to these questions allow the computer to print approximately 100 foundations that should be applied to.

Please understand that applying does not mean automatically being awarded funds. That is what is so unique about the government's program. If you apply, complete the forms properly, and have a need, you will get funds--maybe not scholarships but loans.

In applying for private awards there is no such assurance. Yes, it would be nice to have less loans to repay. And this is why most people use this kind of search. It is also my understanding that Uncle Sam is trying to get one of the MDE's to set up a free search. Someone will have to pay to maintain and update this data bank, who will it be?

If you would like free information about our service write Student College Aid, 7950 N. Stadium Drive #229, Houston, Texas 77030. Ph. 1-800-245-5137 If you use the service, the fee is $49.00

25 COOPERATIVE EDUCATION - AN OVERVIEW

When classroom instruction is combined with on-the-job classroom related work experience, this is called cooperative education. About 100 colleges participate in programs of varying length, scope and administrative style. The employers pay the working students who may be pursuing an Associate, Bachelor's, or Graduate Degree.

Cooperative education began in 1906 at the University of Cincinnati. It spread from there. Some schools, such as Antioch in Ohio, offer strictly cooperative education, i.e. the student attends school for three months and works the following three months.

This section is about cooperative education with the federal government as the employer. The cooperative education coordinator at your college will also have many local businesses participating in this program.

ADVANTAGES

On the average the students earn $6,600 to $9,000 a year for 1,000 hours (graduate students earn more), and the students also have the advantage of continuing their employment at higher than entry-level salaries.

THE LARGEST EMPLOYER

In over 800 campuses, in all states, in the District of Columbia and Puerto Rico the federal government offers the widest choice of employment for various academic majors.

Work sites are as varied as a national park, a downtown federal office building, a military base, or campuses. The federal government offers the widest choice of skills or career fields also. Most are in high demand.

Presently, the federal cooperative education program employs about 14,000 students. Fifteen years ago only 4,000 students were employed.

TYPES OF COOP EDUCATION PROGRAMS

There is great flexibility in scheduling study in on the job training. The final decision for pattern of study and work usually rests with the school. The patterns are: 1. Parallel study and work. The student attends school half a day and reports to the work site for half a day. 2. Alternating. The student attends full classes one school term; the following term he/she works full time. 3. Summer work. This type is not common. The student works only in the summer.

The hourly wage follows the GS pay scale. If student enter the program at the GS2 level, they can expect to earn $6.65 per hour, presently. In following years the students advance and the GS3 level is presently $7.30 per hour and so forth. These figures do not include future cost of living adjustments.

ADVANTAGES FOR THE FEDERAL GOVERNMENT

This program helps the government attract qualified persons for federal service in career areas considered to be in short supply. It encourages student participation in new and developing fields. Equal employment opportunity goals are supported. Situations in which only one sex was employed are alleviated. the government has the opportunity to realistically assess the abilities and attitudes of prospective employees. And finally, it helps the government build understanding among students of federal job and career opportunities.

ADVANTAGES FOR THE STUDENT

The coop education program provides the student with a source of income. The pay schedule into which he/she is classified begins at $6.55 an hour. This is much better than college work-study and summer jobs which usually pay minimum wage.

This program allows the student to make a more informed career choice. the student learns the practicality of academic studies. This program can result in the student's employment with the government in a professional capacity after graduation. Studies have shown that students who took the coop education route and became professionals earn more than their counterparts who took the traditional road.

HOW TO GET INTO THE PROGRAM

HOW TO GET INTO THE PROGRAM

After you are enrolled in a participating college you are eligible to apply for this program. So what you want to do is first identify the career that interest you. Decide which schools having the coop education programs you would like to attend. For detailed information about the federal government program see "EARN & LEARN" by M. Joseph.

APPENDIX A: STATE INFORMATION AGENCIES

Many students try to find their lenders by going through their guarantee agency in their home state or in the state in which they went to college. The name, location etc. is obtained through the State Information Agency.

A question sometime asked us, "If I am in default on my college loans, does this preclude my child from qualifying for governmental monies?"

The answer is "no", but it would preclude him/her from getting a PLUS loan, as this is available through the parent's creditworthiness.

Remember the words of JFK in his inaugural address? "Ask not what your Country can do for you, ask what you can do for your country." One answer is, "Repay your student loans."

Alabama
Student Assistance Program
Alab. Comm on Higher Educ.
One Court Square, Suite 221
Montgomery, AL 36104-0001
(205)269-2700

Alaska
AK Comm on Postsecondry Ed
Box FP, 400 Willoughby
Juneau, AK 99811
(907)465-2962

Arizona
Comm Postsecondary Ed.
2020 N. Central Avenue
Phoenix, AZ 85012
(602)255-3109

Arkansas
Dept of Higher Education
114 E. Capital
Little Rock, AR 72201
(501)324-9300

California
Student Aid Comm
PO Box 510845
Sacramento, CA 94245-0845
(916)445-0880

Colorado
Col Comm on Higher Educ
1300 Broadway, 2nd Fl
Denver, CO 80203
(303)866-2723

Connecticut
DEEPT. of Higher Educ
61 Woodland St.
Hartford, CT 06105
(203)566-2618

Delaware
Dela Postsecondary Ed Comm
State Office Building
820 N. French St.
Wilmington, DE 19801
(302)577-3240

District of Columbia
Office of Postsecondary Ed
Research and Assistance
2100 Martin Luther King Jr. Ave., SE
Washington, DC 20020
(202)727-3685

Florida
Student Financial Assis.
Dept. of Educ.
1344 Florida Education Center
Tallahassee, FL 32399
(904)488-1034

Georgia
Student Finance Authority
2082 East Exchange Pl #200
Tucker, GA 30084
(404)493-5402

Hawaii
Hawaii St Postscndry Ed Comm
Bachman Hall, Room 209
2444 Dole St
Honolulu, HI 96822
(808)948-8213

Idaho
State Board of Education
650 West State St
Boise, ID 83720

(208)334-2270

Illinois
State Scholarship Comm
Client Support Services
106 Wilmot Rd
Deerfield, IL 60015
(708)948-8550

Indiana
State Student Assis Comm
964 N. Pennsylvania Street
Indianapolis, IN 46204
(317)232-2350

Iowa
College Aid Comm
201 Jewett Building
9th & Grand
Des Moines, IA 50309
(515)281-3501

Kansas
Board of Regents, St of Kansas
400 SW 8th St Ste 609 Cptl Twr
Topeka, KS 66603
(913)296-3517

Kentucky
Higher Educ Assis Authority
1050 U S 127 South Ste. 102
West Frankfort Office Complex
Frankford, KY 40601
(502)564-7990

Louisiana
Student Financial Assistance Commission
P O Box 91202

Baton Rouge. LA 70821-9202
(504)922-1011

Maine
Finance Authority of Maine
ME Education Assistance Division
State House Station, #119
One Weston Court
Augusta, ME 04330
(207)289-2183

Maryland
State Scholarship Board
2100 Guilford Ave Rm. 207
Baltimore, MD 21218
(410)333-6420

Massachusetts
Board of Regents of Higher Educ
Scholarship Office
330 Stuart St
Boston, MA 02116
(617)727-9420

Michigan
MI Higher Educ Asst Authority
P O Box 30008
Lansing, MI 48909
(517)373-3394

Minnesota
MN Higher Educ Coord Board
Capitol Square Bldg #400
550 Cedar St
St. Paul, MN 55101
(612)296-3974

Mississippi
Board of Trustees of State Institutions of Higher Learning
Student Financial Aid
3825 Ridgewood Road
Jackson, MS 39211-6453
(601)982-6570

Missouri
Coord Board for Higher Educ
101 Adams St.
Jefferson City, MO 65101
(314)751-2361

Montana
Comm of Higher Educ
35 South Last Chance Gulch
Helena, MT 59620
(406)444-6570

Nebraska
CONTACT INDIVIDUAL SCHOOLS

Nevada
Financial Aid Office
U of NV, Reno
Rm 200 TSSC
Reno, NV 89557
(702)784-4666

New Hampshire
New Hampshire Postsecondary Ed Comm
2 Industrial Park Dr.
Concord, NH 03301-8512
(603)271-2555

New Jersey

Dept of Higher Educ
Office of Student Assis
4 Quakerbridge Plaza CN 540
Trenton, NJ 08625
(609)588-3268, (800)792-8670

New Mexico
Commission on Higher Education
1068 Cerrillos Road
Santa Fe, NM 87501
(505)827-8300

New York
Higher Education Svcs Comm
99 Washington Ave, Rm 1438
Albany, NY 12255
(518)473-0431

North Carolina
State Education Assis Authy
Box 2688
Chapel Hill, NC 27515
(919)549-8614

North Dakota
Student Financial Assis Program
Capitol Bldg, 10th Floor
Bismarck, ND 58505
(701)224-4114

Ohio
Ohio Board of Regents
30 East Broad St, 36th Floor
Columbus, OH 43266-0417
(614)466-7420

Oklahoma
Oklahoma State Regents/Higher

Educ
PO Box 54009
Oklahoma City, OK 73154
(405)521-2444

Oregon
State Scholarship Comm
1445 Willamette St #9
Eugene, OR 97401
(503)346-4166

Pennsylvania
Higher Educ Assis Agency
Towne House, 660 Boas St.
Harrisburg, PA 17102
(717)257-2800,(PA)
(800)692-7435

Rhode Island
Higher Educ Assis Authy
560 Jefferson Blvd.
Warwick, RI 02886
(401)277-2050

South Carolina
SC Tuition Grants Agency
P O Box 12159
Columbia, SC 29211
(803)734-1200

South Dakota
Office of the Secretary
Dept of Educ & Cultural Affairs
700 Governors Drive
Pierre, SD 57501-2291
(605)773-3134

Tennessee
TN Student Assis Corp

404 James Robertson Parkway
Parkway Towers, Ste. 1950
Nashville, TN 37243-0820
(615)741-1346, TN (800)342-1663

Texas
Higher Educ. Coord Board
Box 12788, Capitol Station
Austin, TX 78711
(512)483-6340

Utah
Utah State Board of Regents
335 W.N. Temple, 3 Triad, Ste. 550
Salt Lake City, UT 84180-1205
(801)538-5247

Vermont
Vermont Student Asst. Corp
Champlain Mill, Box 2000
Winooski, VT 05404
(802)655-9602

Virginia
Council of Higher Educ
James Monroe Bldg
101 North 14th St
Richmond, VA 23219
(804)371-7941

Washington
Higher Education Coordinating Board
917 Lake Ridge Way, GV-11
Olympia, WA 98504
(206)753-3571

West Virginia

Higher Educ Grant Program
P O Box 4007
Charleston, WV 25364
(304)347-1211

Wisconsin
State of Wisconsin Higher Educ Aids Bd
PO Box 7885
Madison, WI 53707
(608)267-2206

Wyoming
University of Wyoming
Student Financial Aid
Box 3335, University Station
Laramie, WY 82071
(307)766-2116

Guam
Financial Aid Office
University of Guam
Mangilao, Guam 96923
(617)734-2921, x3657

Puerto Rico
Council on Higher Educ
Box 23305, U.P.R. Station
Rio Piedras, PR 00931
(809)758-3350

Virgin Islands
Board of Education
Commandant Gade,
O.V. No. 11
St. Thomas, VI 00801
(809)774-4546

INDEX

ABROAD PROGRAMS 159
AFFLUENT 121
ASSET SHELTER 94
BANKRUPTCY CLAIMS 68
CAMPUS SECURITY DISCLOSURES 165
CONSOLIDATION OF LOANS 89
COOPERATIVE EDUCATION - AN OVERVIEW 169
CORRESPONDENCE COURSES 151
CREDIT BUREAUS 72
CREDIT BY EXAMINATION 153
DEFAULTED BORROWERS 70
DEFAULTED LOANS 69
DEFENSE OF INFANCY 60
EXPERIENCE/EMPLOYMENT 153
FORBEARANCE 60
FORBEARANCE 83
FOREIGN STUDENTS 157
FSLS AND FPLUS 80
GRADUATE AWARDS 149
HEALTH EDUCATION PROGRAMS 129
HIGH-RISK BORROWERS 68
INCARCERATED STUDENTS 52
INCARCERATED STUDENTS 151
INCOME-SENSITIVE REPAYMENT 83
(JTPA) 154
LOAN SALES AND TRANSFERS 83
MEMBERS OF RELIGIOUS ORDERS 156
MILITARY MEDICAL PROGRAMS 135
MILITARY SCHOLARSHIPS 127
MINORITY PROGRAMS 136
NON-GOVERNMENTAL LOANING SOURCES 102
OVERPAYMENT FOR PELL GRANTS 55
PELL GRANT PROGRAM 52
PERKINS LOAN 59
PROPRIETARY SCHOOLS 160
PUPILS FROM HINDERED SITUATIONS 66
REMEDIAL COURSES 155
REPAYING LOANS 67
REPEATING A COURSE 153

SCHOLARSHIP LOCATOR SERVICE 167
SELECTIVE SERVICE 80
(SEOG) 57
SEXUAL PROTECTION 165
SPECIAL FEDERAL SCHOLARSHIP 125
STAFFORD LOAN PROGRAM 73
STATE GRANTS 96
STATE INFORMATION AGENCIES 172
STATUTE OF LIMITATIONS 72
STUDY ABROAD 58
STUDY ABROAD 52
SUMMER SESSION ALLOWANCE 154
TELECOMMUNICATIONS 153
UNDERGRADUATE SOURCES 139
UNIVERSAL LIFE 94
VETERANS PROGRAMS 138
VETERINARY MEDICINE 55
VIOLATION OF LOAN LIMITS 155
WHAT TO DO WITH ASSETS 93
WORK-STUDY (FWS) PROGRAM 63

SOON TO BE RELEASED

The 2nd expanded and updated edition of "Less Competitive College Grants and Loans" is to be out January 1995.

For sooner delivery call 1-800-245-5137 or fax your purchase order to 1-713-796-9963.

IMPORTANT INFORMATION

Every year thousands of **non-governmental** grants and loans for college students go unclaimed because students who qualify just do not apply, according to D. J. Cassidy, scholarship specialist.

Student College Aid, established in 1980, is also a nationwide, computerized, scholarship locator service with more than $700,000,000 of non-governmental awards in its database. Students are matched to fitting scholarships by supplying pertinent information which is entered into its computer. The matching sources (about 80) plus 30 pages of other valuable award information are mailed to the student who then requests applications from the sources.

Free information and personalized dataform are available to all students. Data such as college major, religious affiliation, ethnic background, etc. are requested on dataform.

The fee for this service is $49.00. The student benefits from a rapid and accurate dispatch of sources he/she probably would never have found on their own. The sooner the student begins his/her search, the more deadlines he/she qualifies for.

Write or call Student College Aid, 7950 N. Stadium Dr. Suite 229, Houston, TX 77030, 1(800)245-5137 or FAX 713 796-9963.

BEST BUY

The "Directory of College Alumni Groups" is your source book for finding the most current catalog of scholarships, donated by alumni, for students of a particular school.

The 8 1/2" X 5 1/2" 230 page paperback book records over 800 colleges and universities and their alumni associations. The user phones or writes the alumni contact at the listed university for the current alumni scholarship catalog and/or the phone number for the contact for the local alumni group. You can then apply for the awards that are similar to your qualifications, or you can talk to local alumni about all sorts of questions you might have about attending that university.

For students trying to gain acceptance to a hard to gain acceptance college, it is of utmost help to use the local alumni representative as an ombudsman. If there is no local club, contact the nearest one. They will make arrangements to meet with you.

For readers of this book, "How to Obtain Maximum College Financial Aid", 4th edition, the price of **"Directory of College Alumni Groups"** is only $10.00, regularly $19.95, plus $3.00 Priority mail. BOOK SATISFACTION GUARANTEED OR YOUR PURCHASE PRICE IS REFUNDED. Texas residents please add $0.66 tax.

Send name, address, **phone #,** check or MC or Visa number & expire date to: Student College Aid Pub Div, 7950 N Stadium Dr # 229, Houston, TX 77030. Or phone 1(800)245-5137 or Fax 1(713)796-9963 .

ORDER TODAY